ROUTLEDGE LIBRARY EDITIONS:
EDUCATION

EDUCATION

EDUCATION
Its Nature and Purpose

M. V. C. JEFFREYS

Volume 144

Routledge
Taylor & Francis Group
LONDON AND NEW YORK

First published in 1971

This edition first published in 2012
by Routledge
2 Park Square, Milton Park, Abingdon, Oxfordshire OX14 4RN

Simultaneously published in the USA and Canada
by Routledge
711 Third Avenue, New York, NY 10017

First issued in paperback 2014

Routledge is an imprint of the Taylor and Francis Group, an informa company

© 1971 George Allen & Unwin Ltd

All rights reserved. No part of this book may be reprinted or reproduced or utilised in any form or by any electronic, mechanical, or other means, now known or hereafter invented, including photocopying and recording, or in any information storage or retrieval system, without permission in writing from the publishers.

Trademark notice: Product or corporate names may be trademarks or registered trademarks, and are used only for identification and explanation without intent to infringe.

British Library Cataloguing in Publication Data
A catalogue record for this book is available from the British Library.

ISBN 13: 978-0-415-69762-0 (Volume 144)
ISBN 13: 978-0-415-75127-8 (pbk)

Publisher's Note
The publisher has gone to great lengths to ensure the quality of this reprint but points out that some imperfections in the original copies may be apparent.

Disclaimer
The publisher has made every effort to trace copyright holders and would welcome correspondence from those they have been unable to trace.

Education:
Its Nature and Purpose

M. V. C. JEFFREYS, C.B.E.

London
GEORGE ALLEN AND UNWIN LTD
RUSKIN HOUSE   MUSEUM STREET

First published in 1971

This book is copyright under the Berne Convention. All
rights are reserved. Apart from any fair dealing for the
purpose of private study, research, criticism or review,
as permitted under the Copyright Act, 1956, no part of this
publication may be reproduced, stored in a retrieval system,
or transmitted, in any form or by any means, electronic, electrical,
chemical, mechanical, optical, photocopying, recording or
otherwise, without the prior permission of the copyright
owner. Inquiries should be addressed to the publishers.

© George Allen & Unwin Ltd 1971

ISBN 0 04 370036 5 *Cased*
     0 04 370037 3 *Paper*

Printed in Great Britain
in 10 point Times Roman
by Cox & Wyman Ltd
London, Fakenham and Reading

'Every man shall count for one, said Bentham, and not more than one: that is the maxim of democracy. Every man shall count for one, and not less than one – that is the maxim of education. The whole issue of the development of true human personality lies in that slight change of phrase.'

        Cyril Norwood: *The English Tradition of Education*, p. 308.

'No one can acquire for another – not one,
 Not one can grow for another – not one.
The song is to the singer, and comes back most to
                                    him,
The teaching is to the teacher, and comes back
                                  most to him.'

        Walt Whitman: *A Song of the Rolling Earth.*

The cover photographs illustrate three of education's many aspects: (*left*) a Koranic school in West Africa; (*centre*) a modern language laboratory; (*right*) part of an examination hall in France, with candidates sitting their Baccalauréat.

Contents

Introduction	*page*	xi
1	THEORY AND PRACTICE	1
2	THE INDIVIDUAL AND SOCIETY	7
3	FREEDOM AND AUTHORITY	24
4	CONTINUITY AND CHANGE: THE NATURE OF GROWTH	42
5	TEACHING AND LEARNING	56
6	FACT AND FEELING: KINDS OF TRUTH	74
7	MORALITY AND RELIGION	97
8	CONCLUSION	117
Index		120

Introduction

'Look out, gentlemen, the schoolmaster is abroad!'
Lord Brougham, addressing the London Mechanics' Institute, 1825.
'I don't know, Ma'am, why they make all this fuss about education.'
Lord Melbourne to Queen Victoria.

These two remarks may be taken, the one positively, the other negatively, to announce the era of public education in this country: in the nineteenth century the gradual establishment of free, compulsory elementary education, and in the present century the great expansion of secondary and higher education.

It is hard to realize, in our own day, the magnitude of the revolution of which the schools were the instrument. It is not only that the mass of people have been taught to read and write, and that the universities are open to talent. What has happened is a social revolution, in which cultural authority has shifted from family and social tradition to the schools. The driving force of that revolution was the application of mechanical power (from the steam-engine to the computer) to industry and commerce. The agency of the social revolution was education.

In a century and a half a stable, predictable society was transformed into an extremely mobile and unpredictable one. The more fluid society becomes, the more does its civilization have to depend explicitly on education rather than implicitly on tradition. H. G. Wells was not overstating the case when he wrote: 'Human history becomes more and more a race between education and catastrophe.' And, when he wrote those words, the possibilities of catastrophe were less obvious than they are now.

No revolution is an unmixed blessing. Educational opportunity, and educational achievement, have divided families against themselves, destroyed the pride based on continuity of occupation, uprooted local loyalties and confused established values. The academic rat-race, by putting a premium on memorized knowledge, has done much to degrade the quality of education itself. Even our language has changed; a new, flat English of the schools, dominated by that dubious tyrant, spelling, has taken the place of the varied English of family, village and county.[1]

---

[1] We may live to see all indigenous forms of English pushed out by mid-Atlantic.

On balance, however, the schools have been the greatest single civilizing agency in our modern national history. We are immeasurably in debt to our teachers, especially the elementary school teachers of the late nineteenth and early twentieth centuries, whose long struggle for basic literacy and the elements of good behaviour was waged in dark, prison-like buildings, amidst poverty, dirt, disease, and hooliganism; with inadequate equipment, large classes, low pay, and scant public recognition.

The purpose of this book is to inquire into the nature and purpose of education. Since education is nothing less than learning to live, the task is not an easy one. For, by definition, the problems of education are the problems of human life. An educated person is one who has made a systematic effort to recognize and come to terms with those problems, not only at the level of intellectual apprehension, but at the level of attitudes and action. This book attempts to distinguish some of these problems.

We can be thankful that, in this country, a broad and generous notion of the scope of education has prevailed. The prescription of the Act of 1944, which laid upon the local authorities the responsibility to 'contribute towards the spiritual, moral, mental, and physical development of the community', was no novel idea. Our schools have traditionally concerned themselves with a good deal more than academic instruction. Milton's famous definition: 'I call therefore a complete and generous education that which fits a man to perform justly, skilfully and magnanimously all the offices both private and public of peace and war', reminds us that education is moral and practical as well as intellectual and academic, vocational as well as liberal.

Education, like democracy, is a slow and hazardous business. It can go wrong, and it can fail. We gain nothing by entertaining illusions about the efficacy of education. We believe in education, as we believe in democracy, because the alternative is ultimate despair of humanity. But neither education nor democracy can be better than the people engaged in them.

Chapter 1
Theory and Practice

The theory of education draws upon a number of academic disciplines. Philosophy, psychology, sociology, history are some of them. This series of books includes volumes on these disciplines. The purpose of this introductory book is to examine what education means, and to do so in a way that does not lose sight of teachers and pupils – and parents, for that matter – as people.

'Training', as a description of the professional preparation of teachers for their job, has become a dirty word, recalling the inadequate – though heroic – efforts of last century to equip ill-educated young people with enough tricks of the trade to enable them to hold their own in a classroom in the struggle to pass on what education they had to the next generation.

'Training Colleges' have become 'Colleges of Education'; and we like to think of them as places where intending teachers can extend their own personal education, with the necessary professional slant. The extension of the college course from two years to three, advocated in the McNair Report of 1944 and implemented in 1960, has given the colleges more opportunity to educate, as well as train, their students. But, while on one side of the fence we talk of the education of intending teachers, there has been some grumbling from the schools that the colleges are turning out teachers with airy-fairy notions who do not know how to mark a register.

The truth is that proficiency in every art – whether it be painting, music, or teaching – involves training, but also needs more than training. Training cannot produce genius; but genius can profit from training. Inspiration is the reward of hard work, not a substitute for it. Teaching has its techniques as much as any other art. And the process of acquiring those techniques is training.

It is equally true that good teaching involves more than competent technique. The good teacher has at least two other things besides technical competence. One of these is some sense of vocation. The teacher must believe the job to be worth doing for its own sake; and he must want to do it. The other desideratum is that the teacher should himself be an educated person – literate, civilized, knowledgeable, thoughtful, humane, self-reliant.[1]

[1] How far our higher education is successful will always be debatable. And, fortunately, an individual's education does not end with three years at

The question may be asked: Why must we concern ourselves with *theory* of education? Why can we not just get on with the job of educating the young, and pick up the tricks of the trade as we go? Education was going on, and going on successfully, centuries before anyone thought of training teachers. Is the modern vogue for educational theory (with all the institutional organization, plant, and personnel that go with it) anything more than a bid for prestige by getting on to the technological band-waggon?[1]

It is true that, although the education of the young has been studied systematically since Vittorino da Feltre, and before that by Quintilian and Cicero, Aristotle and Plato, there was no systematic training of teachers in this country until 1811 (when the National Society was founded and the pupil-teacher system began). Training Colleges proper owe their origin to Sir James Kay-Shuttleworth (Battersea College was founded in 1840). The earliest European teacher-training was in Prussia in the second half of the seventeenth century.

In the past century and a half, teacher-training in this country has made enormous progress. The standards of training, and indirectly the status of the teaching profession, have gained greatly from the increasingly close connection between the colleges and the universities. The first important step was the establishment of the Joint Examination Boards, in about 1930, each consisting of representatives of the university and of the colleges concerned. The Joint Board scheme, however, created no more than an examinational connection between the universities and the colleges. Then the McNair Report of 1944 recommended that the universities should take much more responsibility for the training of teachers, and that the colleges should be related to their regional universities in organizations (usually called Institutes of Education) which should do a great deal more than merely conduct examinations. Within an Institute of Education much fruitful co-operation between colleges and university, including the

---

[1] How formidable educational technology is becoming can be judged by looking at some recent books, such as E. Stones: *Readings in Educational Psychology* (Methuen, 1970). Perhaps the reader can draw some comfort from the following passage on programmed learning (if he can make out what it means): 'The early vogue for programs based on the operant conditioning of verbal behaviour and emphasis on hardware is giving way to an open questioning approach which emphasizes the precise statement of objectives and the analysis of the teaching task from the logical and the psychological point of view.'

---

college or university. At the same time, when one hears a first-class honours graduate, in a television interview, say 'summink' for 'something', one is mildly shocked.

promotion of research, could and did take place in the twenty years following the McNair Report. The Robbins Report of 1963 recommended, among other things, that the colleges should come fully into the university orbit (i.e. financially and administratively as well as academically). This would have been a logical development, and would have benefited both the colleges and the universities. For various reasons this further step has not been taken.[1]

To return to the question: Why theory of education? The answer, quite simply, is that one is more likely to achieve something if one knows what one is trying to do and how one proposes to do it. Without theory the moon-landing would have been impossible. Without musical theory, each effort in composition would have to start from scratch. Theory, after all, is the rational aspect of practice, the light of experience cast upon yet untrodden paths. It is true that, in the course of development of any art, a great deal of empirical know-how is accumulated, and that this is 'theory', though perhaps not systematized. But in every art a stage of development is reached when implicit know-how is not enough, and theory has to be explicitly organized.

If we are to live intelligently, we need a theory not only for this or that particular enterprise or kind of activity, but for life as a whole. We need, if we may use an old-fashioned term, a philosophy of life. Moreover, since education is the business of learning how to live, our theory of education must be of a piece with our general philosophy of life.

Here, however, comes the rub. What we believe about the nature, purpose, and means of education is inseparable from what we believe about life in general – that is, if our thinking is to have coherence and integrity. It is therefore impossible to propose a theory of education without, implicitly or explicitly, declaring one's general philosophy of life.

There is no need to look beyond the list of chapter headings to see that this book is planned and worked out in terms of a number of tensions or conflicts: between the individual and society, between freedom and authority, between continuity and change and, finally, between man's struggle towards perfection and his continual failure and frustration – the fundamental contradiction of human existence imaged in the Greek myth of Sisyphus, and most fully and profoundly elaborated in Christian theology.[2]

[1] Two of these reasons were: (*a*) reluctance of the local authorities to relinquish administrative control of their colleges; and (*b*) reluctance of the universities, at a time of rapid expansion, to take on even bigger responsibilities.

[2] See Albert Camus: *The Myth of Sisyphus*. In our own day the Existentialists are acutely aware of the deep human problems which an easy enthusiasm for modern technology invites us to forget.

Struggle, tension and conflict are, I believe, inevitably part of the human condition. Human society is not self-perfectible – not self-perfectible, that is, by any knowledge or skills that we yet possess. A hundred years ago many people sincerely believed that coal, iron and steam were going to usher in the millennium. They were wrong. Today our technical means of controlling our environment are immeasurably more sophisticated. But optimism is very much more cautious, if indeed our generation can be described as optimistic at all. We talk less of progress than our grandparents and great-grandparents did. And we make apprehensive prognostications (which they would not have understood) that our civilization may blow itself up, poison itself, or (if the permissive society erodes all discipline) die of boredom.

Conflict is inevitable. But it can also be creative. All creation springs from the tension between what is and what might be. Conflict can, and should, be seen as a positively necessary part of life. This view rejects the notion of the ideal society as a well-oiled machine. It is a view that values many things (including social élites of various kinds) which egalitarians would like to get rid of, and which sees social unity as a highly complex thing, very different from uniformity. It is a view which has no use for a negative idea of virtue; peace is not the absence of war; love is not inoffensiveness; fellowship is not non-interference.

Such a view is not a currently popular one. The more popular creed, despite the apprehensiveness inspired by the unpredictability of the new God, Technology, is that technology will turn up trumps in the end. Just a little more scientific knowledge and all will be well, in a smooth, classless, affluent Utopia. But, although the background of this book is a view of life which is not currently popular, it is a view that has its roots in our long Hebrew-Christian and Graeco-Roman tradition.[1]

It is only fair that the writer of a book of this kind should put his cards on the table. This does not mean that the book has no message for those who hold different beliefs about the nature and destiny of man. I would maintain the contrary. The facts of life are the same, though they look different from different angles. The problems of education (of growth, learning, forming attitudes) are the same problems, though there will always be disagreement – and I would say that such disagreement is healthy – about the methods of dealing with them. What this book seeks to do is to present the main problems of education in such a way as to

[1] Readers who want a fuller statement of this view of life would profit by studying Professor G. H. Bantock's admirable book, *T. S. Eliot and Education* (Faber and Faber, 1970). It was Eliot who said: 'A mob will be no less a mob if it is well fed, well clothed, well housed, and well disciplined.' That remark has some considerable educational implications.

help the reader, whatever his personal beliefs, to clarify his ideas about them. The author's disclosure of his own beliefs will, I hope, help rather than hinder the reader in knowing where he stands and in making up his own mind. For he can make allowance for the author's personal standpoint.

It may well be that other volumes in this series will be written from standpoints other than my own. That would be all to the good, provided the reader can steer his own course. It is after all, part of education to navigate among the currents and winds of opinion, and so work out one's own passage to the truth. To this end, we must at any time have reasoned grounds for action – because events have to be taken as they come, and will not wait for us to re-think our philosophy. Yet we must also continually believe that we may be mistaken, and be ready if necessary to change our opinions. As John Milton wrote three hundred years ago: 'He who thinks we are to pitch our tent here, and have attained the utmost prospect of reformation which this mortal glass wherein we contemplate can show us, ... that man by this very opinion declares that he is yet far short of truth.' And again: 'The light which we have gained was given us, not to be ever staring on, but by it to discover onward things more remote from our knowledge.'[1]

BIBLIOGRAPHY

ARCHAMBAULT, R. D. (ed.), *Philosophical Analysis and Education* (Routledge and Kegan Paul, 1966).
BANTOCK, G. H., *Education and Values* (Faber and Faber, 1965).
BANTOCK, G. H., *T. S. Eliot and Education* (Faber and Faber, 1970).
BRUBACHER, J. S., *A History of the Problems of Education* (McGraw-Hill, 1947).
ELVIN, H. L., *Education and Contemporary Society* (C. A. Watts, 1965).
HARDIE, C. D., *Truth and Fallacy in Educational Theory* (C.U.P., 1942).
HOLLINS, T. H. B. (ed.), *Aims in Education* (Manchester University Press, 1964).
JACKS, M. L., *Total Education* (Routledge and Kegan Paul, 1946).
JEFFREYS, M. V. C., *Glaucon, An Enquiry into the Aims of Education* (Pitman, 1950; revised 1955; reprinted 1961).
JUDGES, A. V. (ed.), *Education and the Philosophic Mind* (Harrap, 1957).
MORRISH, I., *Disciplines of Education* (Allen and Unwin, 1967).
PETERS, R. S. (ed.), *The Concept of Education* (Routledge and Kegan Paul, 1967).

[1] John Milton: *Areopagitica*.

REID, L. A., *Philosophy and Education* (Heinemann, 1962).
ROSS, J. S., *Groundwork of Educational Theory* (Harrap, 1952).
RUSK, R. R., *Doctrines of the Great Educators* (Macmillan, 2nd Edition 1954).
RUSK, R. R., *The Philosophical Bases of Education* (University of London Press, 1928; 2nd Edition 1956).
SCHEFFLER, I., *Philosophy and Education* (Allyn and Bacon, Boston, 1958).
SCHEFFLER, I., *The Language of Education* (C. C. Thomas, Illinois, 1960).
THOMSON, G. H., *A Modern Philosophy of Education* (Allen and Unwin, 1929).
TIBBLE, J. W. (ed.), *The Study of Education* (Routledge and Kegan Paul, 1966).
WHITEHEAD, A. N., *The Aims of Education* (Benn, 1962).

Chapter 2
The Individual and Society

Tension and conflict are inescapable facts of experience. A basic tension is the two-way pull towards individuality on the one hand and social conformity on the other.

We value our individuality. We want to be different from other people. We like to be recognized as ourselves, with our own characteristics, interests, tastes and abilities. Names mean a good deal to us, because they symbolize our distinct individuality. If we no longer had names, but numbers, we should feel that we had lost something of our personal identity. If people remember our names, we are pleased. One of the important social accomplishments of men and women in public life is the ability to recall the names of the people they meet.

There is a deep need in each person to be unique, and to develop his uniqueness. Yet this personal identity is a mysterious thing. We are always changing, and yet we remain ourselves. The material that our bodies are made of is continually being replaced. And yet I remain I, and you remain you. What is it that holds together, organizes, the elements we are made of, so that we change, grow, and yet remain ourselves? How much of the body can change without personal identity being destroyed? This question takes on fresh meaning in an age of kidney- and heart-transplants. What convoluted emotions lie behind the reluctance of a white patient to receive the heart of a coloured donor? Or, from a different angle, if a body is kept alive after irreparable brain damage, how far can we say that he or she is the same person?

However that may be, we want to be individuals. Advertisers cash in on our desire to be 'different' – by selling us all the same things! A photograph of an assembly of people at a conference is very different from a photograph of rows of cars that have come off the assembly line. That is how it should be. People should be unique. Cars of a certain make should be identical.

Nevertheless, important as our uniqueness is to us, we do not want to be too 'different'. It is disconcerting to meet extreme differences of habits and customs, outlooks and ideas. To get on comfortably with people we must have a good deal in common with them. The paradoxical truth is that the personal individuality we value so much is absolutely dependent upon our belonging to a community or communities. Without social membership, and all that this means in terms of adjustment, concession, emulation, love, hate, and so on, we should never become properly human at all. There are enough records of feral children (human children brought up in a non-human environment) to show that our very humanity remains unawakened without human contact. When Aristotle said: 'Man is a political animal', he was simply stating this basic fact of life – that the proper growth of a human being can take place only in the 'polis' or organized community. The question which came first, individual or society, is a hen-and-egg question and quite profitless. When Aristotle went on to say that the number of citizens in the 'polis' should not be more than could be taken in at a single view, he was making the point that the sense of membership and loyalty tends to wear thin as numbers increase. Our families, our villages or towns, our countries, mean more to us than the United Nations or the World; though mass communications, especially television, have done something to bring remote people and things closer to us.

It would be misleading to suggest that the tension between individual and society occurs only at the human level. All gregarious animals develop some system of priorities. There are the leaders and the led. Hens have their pecking order. Stags fight for mastery of their stamping-grounds and lordship of their harems of hinds. Anyone who has kept a number of dogs, and studied them intimately, will know how, in a group of several dogs, each will come to have a distinct role. One perhaps is elderly, and has abdicated leadership to Number Two Dog, while keeping his dignity by the occasional growl at anyone who takes a liberty. Another is the *enfant terrible* of the group, tolerated so long as he is not too much of a nuisance. And so on. Animals, no less than humans, need social relations in order to develop their characters. And, in the process of evolving social relations, there is conflict. We also notice that there is most conflict among animals of higher intelligence, and least among those, like bees and ants, whose social organization is dictated by blind instinct. If this is true, it is not surprising that man is the most belligerent of animals. The other side of that coin is that man and the higher animals have more mutual affection. It is difficult to imagine a love affair in an ants' nest.

If we ask what is the end or goal of a human being's development, we shall need a word to denote something more than is conveyed by the word 'individual'. The word we need is 'person' or 'personal'. An earthworm is an individual, living organism. But it does not live at what we would regard as a personal level. Would we regard a dog as a 'person'? The question is at least debatable. What is quite certain is that we do expect a fully developed human being to have the qualities implied by the word 'person'.

What then do we mean by 'person' and 'personal'? Unique identity is part of what we mean, but only part. The word has at least two other implications. One of these is what we may call rational and moral responsibility. We expect a person to take responsibility for what he is and says and does. That is part of what the word means, and we could not apply it to a creature, like a bee or an ant, whose behaviour is blindly instinctive. If we say that behaviour at the personal level is rational and moral, we do not mean that persons are invariably rational and moral. There would be very few persons in the world if that were so. What we mean is that, to merit the label 'person', an individual must at least understand what rational and moral behaviour is. We demand that he should be the self-acknowledged author of his behaviour, that he should put his signature to his work. Behaviour that is purely instinctive, or purely imitative, we would not recognize as 'personal'.

The third implication of the word 'person' is fellowship with other persons. One cannot be a person *in vacuo*. Personal living involves the sharing of one's life with other persons, with mutual respect for one another's freedom and responsibility. In Martin Buber's words: 'All real living is meeting', the communication of person with person: that is to say, fellowship. Or, as Kant put it, we should treat other people as ends in themselves and never as means to our own ends. This respect of person for person is the basis of any acceptable morality. Lying and stealing are wrong, sexual exploitation is wrong, violence and murder are wrong, because these things mean using other people, abusing or exploiting other people, damaging or destroying other people, for our own advantage.

The argument so far can be summarized as follows: The full personal development of a human being involves the cultivation of individuality and also of social relations. In the individual–society nexus, each side needs the other. But in the working out of interpersonal relations in any community, there is bound to be tension and even conflict. Only in an inconceivably ideal state of things, where (to use Rousseau's terms) the general will was the will of all, would there be no conflict. Nor is it at all certain that we should like that sort of ideal harmony, even if we could have it. The Communion of Saints might turn out to be a crashing bore. At all events, in the world as we know it, where it is difficult to separate effort from conflict, there is bound to be tension. There is a kind of love-hate relationship between each and all. We need one another, and yet we get in one another's way. A profound truth that emerges from our experience of social tension is the paradoxical relation between giving and getting. Experience teaches us that true gain, in terms of personal growth and fulfilment, comes from giving, not from seeking to get. Selflessness is self-fulfilling; greed is self-frustrating. To most of us glimpses of that truth are vouchsafed, so that we can begin to understand at least the direction in which the solution of life's problem lies. But for most of us the ultimate horizon is a long way off.

In the world as we know it there is bound to be tension and conflict. The very existence of the 'State' (i.e. organized government) is evidence of the need to control by force situations that cannot sort themselves out by spontaneous good will – either because they are so complicated that systematic organization is needed, or because, in every society, there are rogue elements that need the discipline of the law.

We cannot think of the 'State' without also thinking about 'public opinion'. While the State exerts formal control through the various instruments of government (legislation, the armed forces, the Civil Service, the law courts, the police) a great deal of informal control is exercised by public opinion. In a sense public opinion is more powerful than government, for no government can for any length of time run counter to the prevailing climate of opinion, or exceed what public opinion will support. Even if what appears on the face of it to be an intolerable tyranny is nevertheless tolerated, the explanation must be that most people think it a lesser evil than, say, hopeless rebellion or suicide. Apart from extreme cases, there is a normal relation between government and public opinion which we all take for granted. A clear and topical example of the intimate relation between government and public opinion is provided by the recent history of censorship.

The 'State' and 'public opinion' are both abstract terms, and abstractions are always dangerous. On the one hand, without the simplification of abstraction we could not think at all. Without generalization one cannot reason. On the other hand, having made an abstraction, we tend to make an idol of it, endowing it with a life of its own. In other words, in what sense do 'public opinion' and the 'State' exist at all, outside our own minds?

The State is more than the machinery of government. The machinery of government may continue to exist, on paper, when actual government has broken down in revolutionary chaos. Which is a reminder that the State implies not only the existence of governmental machinery but also the functioning of that machinery – that is to say, the activities of everyone in the public service from the Head of State to the newest recruit to the typing pool in a government office. It is difficult, perhaps impossible, to stretch the imagination to encompass all the concrete realities that underlie the abstraction, the State; but the attempt is a salutary exercise.[1]

[1] Those who are interested in the complexity of governmental processes are recommended to consult *Decision in Government*, by Dr Jeremy Bray, M.P. (Gollancz, 1970).

In the case of 'public opinion', it is one thing to use the term glibly as if it meant something, but another thing to explain what the term really does mean. In what sense can we say that a 'consensus' of opinion exists on a particular topic? Even if we could carry out a hundred-per-cent referendum, so that every member of the public was recorded as a 'Yes', a 'No', or a 'Don't know', we should still have only a very crude indication of what people really thought. *Quot homines tot sententiae.* Among fifty million people there are in truth fifty million opinions, none of them absolutely identical. But it is impossible to deal statistically with fifty million individual statements. Therefore we have to generalize, and think and talk in terms of a public opinion which we know is unreal, but to which the realities approximate, more or less. There are times in the history of nations – for example, in this country at the time of the Battle of Britain – when there clearly exists, for practical purposes, an overwhelming consensus of opinion – especially if there is a valiant and eloquent leader to express and confirm it. But on most public issues it is not easy to estimate public opinion. How far are we entitled to say that Americans are tired of the war in Vietnam, or that opinion in our own country is in favour of permissiveness in sex matters? On many problems of undoubted importance, most people simply do not have the knowledge to form a clear opinion; the Common Market is an obvious example. Moreover, in any system of representative government, it is never easy to know whether a vote in the legislature really reflects the balance of opinion in the country at large; the issue of capital punishment is an example.

If the last two paragraphs seem to have laboured the difficulty of identifying the concrete realities corresponding with the abstract terms, the State and public opinion, their justification lies in the importance of not being deceived by our own mental shorthand. We have to use terms like the 'State', 'society', and 'public opinion'. But we ought to know what we are doing when we use them.

To return to the main line of argument: it has been suggested that, in all actual societies, individuals are both dependent upon the society for their very existence, and also in some sense resisting the pressures of society upon them. A notable feature of our modern technological civilization is the enormous, and dangerous, increase of this tension between the individual and organized society. On the one hand, education, higher wages, and leisure, combine to encourage individuality as never before. We tend to forget that, only a century and a half ago, most people had virtually no *choice* at all – of occupation, place of residence, or leisure activities. If you were born in a mining village, or a mill-town, you went down the mine or into the mill; your only recreation was the pub; and you had no holidays. All that has changed. Yet, on the other hand, the coming of large-scale economic and political organization, the umbrella social services (though there are holes in the umbrella), and the bewilderment of the mass media of entertainment and advertisement, combine to push the individual around until he has no life of his own. Even in areas where choice nominally operates, it is nullified by mass-production: package holidays, and commercial products which differ in name but not in substance.

The individual is looked after as never before. But he may get punch-drunk from being pushed around for his own good. There is a real danger of human beings becoming the material of 'social engineering': of people being treated as units, things. The modern problem of social drop-outs (for example, a group of young people seeking to raise £20,000 to buy an island) is an indication of a desire to escape from the over-organization of modern society.

Even if the Welfare State worked perfectly, there would be many who wanted to escape from it. But in fact there are many casualties of imperfect social machinery. To take one actual example, of a young mother with two small children, deserted by her husband. Her National Assistance Book has run out, and her husband has failed to send her any money, although there is a court order that he should do so. She telephones the Probation Department, from which she has had help and advice in the past. They tell her to ring the Ministry of Social Security. She does so, and is told to send in a form of application for a new book. This transaction will take several days, and she says: 'I have no money.' She is told that the only alternative is to go to the offices of the Ministry of Social Security in the nearest town. She replies: 'How can I make a fifty pence journey with two small children when I have no money?' Some time later she learnt from the County Welfare Department that immediate help might have been obtained by applying to her doctor, or to the police, or to the Welfare Department itself. But she did not know this at the time. It is worth noting, perhaps, that the Welfare Departments are less bound by regulations, and more free to use initiative, than, for example, the Ministry of Social Security.

The point of such an example is that, except for the absconding husband, nobody was animated by ill-will. A good deal of the world's misery is caused, not by envy, hatred, malice, and all uncharitableness, but by conscientious people doing their duty according to Section III (g), Para. 9 of the Regulations. That is the price we have to pay for the Welfare State. And it is, incidentally, a forcible reminder of a fact that Sir William Beveridge hammered home some years ago in his book, *Voluntary Action*, namely: that there is still plenty of opportunity for voluntary agencies to supplement the work of the public services.

Enough has been said to make it clear that, when we talk about the individual and society, we must not think of 'society' as a single thing, or uniform substance. Each individual in fact belongs to many societies, within one another, overlapping one another: family, school, neighbourhood, nation, and so on. Broadly speaking, the larger the social unit, the less real it seems, because it is more remote. It was suggested earlier that radio and television had done something to bring distant places and problems closer to us. To some extent this is obviously true. Pictures of starving children, or corpses in Vietnam, have an actuality which mere words cannot convey. But, less obviously, there may be an opposite effect. We watch so many fictional films of violence and crime, which move us only superficially, that there is perhaps a danger of starving children and Vietnam becoming as unreal to us as a Western film or 'Monty Python's Flying Circus'.

One of the dangers of using the abstraction 'society', as if it were something that existed independently, over and against you and me, is that it tempts one to forget the you-and-me relation. In this more concrete and intimate sense, 'society' is the chap next door, in fact my neighbour. Apart from the requirements of the law, what is my duty to my neighbour? And his duty towards me? How, if at all, does the Golden Rule (do to others as you would they should do to you) apply in this actual, imperfect world? Is our guiding principle that of selflessly seeking the good of others, that of looking after our own interests (because, if we don't, nobody will), or some sort of compromise between the two?

This question raises the whole problem of moral obligation, which is discussed in a later chapter. For the moment it is enough to note that all coherent communities recognize moral obligation as between their members; and that there is fairly general agreement that the 'ought' implicit in moral obligation is something *sui generis*, which is not adequately conveyed in the concepts of natural instinct or expediency. That is to say, most people would agree that when I say: 'This is what I *ought* to do', I mean something other than: 'This is what I would like to do', or: 'This would be convenient', or even: 'This would benefit many people'. The essential distinction perhaps is that the last three alternatives indicate *optional* situations, in which I reserve the decision. The essence of the 'ought', or moral imperative, is that it is not optional. Once I see what I ought to do, my only alternative to doing it is to be disgusted with myself for not doing it. In the very recognition of the 'ought' my own ego is superseded and a higher authority takes over. The attitude is summed up in Luther's famous words, 'Ich kann nicht anders'. Or, in modern parlance, 'If I didn't go through with it, I couldn't live with myself'. That is what 'ought' means. When Luther faced the Diet of Worms, or Cranmer went to the stake, these were voluntary acts which need not have been done. But it would be straining the ordinary meaning of words to say that these men *wanted* to do these things. ('If it be Thy will, let this cup pass from me!')

It is of course possible, and legitimate, to deny the proposition that the moral imperative is something other than, and superseding, natural impulse, convenience, or whatever. We can, if we like, dismiss the category of moral obligation as an illusion. We can, with the Logical Positivists, say that moral statements are ways of expressing our feelings, but are unverifiable and therefore strictly meaningless. But, if we do so, we ought (if the use of the word is permissible!) to apply the principle of economy of hypotheses, and give up using a term which is nothing but a pompous version of something else. Not only would this scaling down of vocabulary be difficult in the context of traditional thought; but we should also have to offer some plausible explanation of the curious fact that a totally meaningless category had somehow intruded itself into our thinking, *seeming* to have a meaning which we now decide is meaningless.

Most people think it is more sensible to accept the moral imperative at its face value. It is this moral imperative that undergirds all reasonable human behaviour and social organization, and is (imperfectly) expressed in law and opinion.

It remains to consider what implications this discussion has for education. But, before examining the function of education in relation to the individual and society, there is a more fundamental question to be asked, namely: to what extent does a system of education simply reflect society as it is, and to what extent can education be an instrument of social change? If education does no more than conserve and transmit a particular culture and social order, there is little point in discussing it, since by hypothesis it can do nothing but preserve whatever exists.

Every modern society believes in education as a potent instrument of social change, and for that reason attaches great importance to its schools. In the democracies the prevailing view is that education should be 'open-ended', in the sense that it should produce people capable of thinking for themselves and dedicated to truth wherever it is to be found. In the dictatorships the function of education is rather to stamp all citizens with the orthodox political doctrine – though no doubt educators in the totalitarian countries would repudiate this cynical opinion. We might say that the ideal of democracy is to encourage individual development to the greatest extent that is consistent with social cohesion, while the totalitarian regimes are more ready to subordinate individuals to the collective efficiency of the community. In the present connection, however, the important thing is that the world of today, on both sides of the Iron Curtain, believes in education as an instrument of social progress.

The universality of this modern belief in the power of education should not blind us to the fact that, historically, it is of comparatively recent growth. In societies where change is, or was, very slow, or where life is so hard that survival is a main concern, the function of education must be conservative – either because change is not expected, or because conservation is in itself a difficult enough achievement.

The first clear manifesto in favour of education as an instrument of social change is to be found, about 400 BC, in the writings of Plato. The Sophists before him had opened the way for this view of education by their doctrine that virtue could be taught, and was therefore not entirely dependent on inborn qualities.[1] Plato, however, may be reckoned the first great revolutionary educational thinker. Not satisfied with the purely conservative function of education, nor with the existing state of society, he envisaged the regeneration of society by means of education. For the first time education was seen as something socially creative.

Plato's vision was handicapped in two ways. In the first place, it was only a vision, not a practical programme. Nor did it ever really commend itself to the educated public opinion of his day. The chief indictment brought against Socrates was that he had been unconventional and had corrupted the youth of Athens by teaching disrespect of the Gods (i.e. of the established order). The prevailing opinion in Athens, expressed by Aristotle, was that the business of education was to produce citizens in conformity with the social order.

Secondly, Plato's view involved the logical paradox that, while the perfect system of education was necessary to produce the perfect society, the perfect society was a necessary precondition of the perfect education. To point to this paradox is no criticism of Plato; for it is inseparable from all thinking about education in relation to society. On the one hand, the educational system of any society is limited by the total cultural quality of that society; a society gets the education it deserves, just as it gets the government it deserves. On the other hand, education (at all levels, from nursery to adult) is the only means by which a society can become better. There is no theoretical escape from this logical impasse; it is one of those problems that have to be worked out at the practical level. In point of fact, a society that takes education seriously, and cares

---

[1] These novel views must have been stimulated by the coming of democracy in Athens – though it must be remembered that Greek democracy never extended beyond the body of enfranchised citizens; the notion that slaves could merit full human status is a Christian conception.

enough about it to give it the priority it deserves, is on the way to becoming a better society.

Greek and Roman education remained essentially conservative. Still more so had been the educational systems of ancient India and China. Throughout the Middle Ages in Europe the same is generally true.

At this point we can turn to the question whether the purpose of education is to encourage the development of the individual, or to satisfy the needs of society, and to what extent these two aims conflict. It has been said that the 'recognition of the importance of individual variation from the norm of the group was not only a step forward in educational aims; it was itself the very seed principle from which Western educational progress was to issue'.[1] In ancient and medieval times education was thought of mainly as a means of shaping individuals to fit their appointed roles in society as it was. Such a sweeping generalization needs qualifying. The citizens of a Greek city state, relieved of their chores by slave labour, and with opportunity to practise the arts and to talk about everything under the sun, must in fact have cultivated individuality to a high degree, though this was not the avowed aim of their education. Pericles' Funeral Speech praised the initiative, resource and adaptability of the Athenians.

Again, Christianity, with its proclamation of the equal worth of all human beings, regardless of race or social position, was bound in the long run to raise the status of the individual as such. *Paedeia,* the word used by St Paul in Ephesians vi. 1-4, means the whole process of cultivating the growing personality. Among the Christian Fathers, Augustine, doubtless remembering his own childhood, recognized the child's own 'free curiosity' as a necessary condition of learning. 'No one does well against his will.' This Christian emphasis had to no small extent been anticipated by the Hebrews, who valued children and family life more than any other ancient people, and regarded education as something which all children ought to have. Until the Hellenistic period, Jewish education was given in the home by the father.

It is extremely difficult to assess the contribution of Christianity to our modern educational ideals and practice. It is easy to argue that Christianity has made only a limited impact. The early Christian communities were mostly poor, and also looked for an other-worldly fulfilment of their spiritual hopes, accepting the mundane order of the Roman Empire. Throughout the Middle Ages, although schools and universities were founded, it cannot be claimed that education did much to give effect to the Christian doctrine of man. By the time the Church was powerful enough to organize education, it had lost its early visionary enthusiasm

[1] J. S. Brubacher: *A History of the Problems of Education* (McGraw-Hill, 1947), p. 3.

and evangelical zeal, and accepted the contemporary view of society as a complicated, hierarchical structure into which individuals had to fit as best they could. The other-worldly element survived in monasticism; and medieval chivalry (which was the Church's way of civilizing feudalism) is evidence of some considerable influence of the Christian ethic in secular life; but its aim was to produce a type rather than individuals. Admirable as Jesuit education was in many ways, it did not encourage individual divergence from the set path.

We must remember, however, that the leavening of human society by the Christian spirit has been limited in two important ways, one internal and one external to the Church. On the one hand, the Church in history has faced two ways. As the Body of Christ the Church has stood for the remaking of society as of individual human beings. Thus, in more modern times, Christians worked to rescue the children from the factory system and to provide schools. But, as a pillar of the Establishment, the Church has stood for the existing social order, which included keeping the lower classes in their place and educating them no more than was necessary to secure docility. It is this vested-interest aspect of the historical Church that explains the curious fact that, as at the time of the French Revolution, secular and even anti-clerical forces have proclaimed and fought for political and educational ideals which could never have existed without Christianity.

On the other hand, the task confronting the Church has at all times (from the breakdown of the Roman Empire to the rise of the modern technological society) been extremely difficult; and there is nothing surprising in the fact that Christian efforts to reform the world have been only partially successful. If Christian theology has anything to tell us, it is that the Christian life, individual and social, is very difficult, and that human nature, while aware of its dire need of redemption, is at all times perversely resistant to the Grace of God. What ought to surprise the historian is not how little but how much influence Christianity has had on human history.

Indeed, without Christianity, it is impossible to imagine the modern world at all. Without Christianity, there would have been no light in the darkness when the Roman Empire disintegrated, no power to civilize the barbarians, no Twelfth-Century Renaissance, no Fifteenth-Century Renaissance, no Reformation, no modern science, no modern democracy, no Welfare State, no basic human rights, and (since Marxism is in a sense Christian theology upside-down) no Communism.

Underlying this problem of evaluating the influence of Christianity in history is the deeper question whether the Kingdom of God can in any circumstances come to earth – that is to say, whether human society is perfectible within the framework of time and space. The main tradition of Christian thought would maintain that, while the temporal order and the spiritual order interpenetrate one another, and the spiritual order can continually leaven and partially redeem the temporal order, the dualism of the two can never be wholly overcome in mundane history. The medieval Papacy made a grand effort to unite the two orders, but the success of the Renaissance and Reformation were the measure of the ultimate failure of the medieval synthesis.[1]

The Western world had to go through many centuries of its history before the value and needs of the individual as such were systematically embodied in education. And even now the process is far from complete. Two conditions had to be fulfilled before what we know as 'child-centred education' could win general acceptance. One of these conditions is a matter of belief; the other is a matter of organization.

A number of influences contributed to create a belief in the obligation to give every child, irrespective of wealth and status, the fullest possible opportunity to develop his abilities. The Renaissance affirmed (or rather, reaffirmed[2]) the wholeness of man, body and soul. The Reformation emphasized the responsibility of the individual and (in secular affairs) encouraged enterprise. Later came the philosophical ferment that provided the ideology of the French Revolution. One ingredient in the ferment was the rationalist, critical spirit that left nothing unquestioned and therefore refused to accept the *status quo* as part of the eternal order of things. Another main ingredient was the new belief in Nature: that man is naturally good and that he fulfils his destiny by following his own nature rather than by obedience to a transcendental or other authority. It was Condorcet's dream that Nature, governed by Reason, could perfect man and human society. The American Declaration of Independence, proclaiming that 'all men are created equal', was inspired by the French revolutionary philosophy, which in turn produced the French Declaration of the Rights of Man. The way was now open to the reforming movements of the nineteenth century, in every political and social field.

Without an established system of schools, no educational doctrine can be widely adopted. The second main condition of modern methods of education was the foundation of national systems of education.

In the development of national systems of education some of the Continental countries were ahead of Britain. Even our own John Locke had more influence abroad than at home. The earliest practical impact

---

[1] See Jacques Maritain: *True Humanism* (Bles, 1938), especially Chapter III: *The Christian and the World*.

[2] Renaissance Humanism was preceded by the Christian Humanism of Thomas Aquinas, restated in our day by Jacques Maritain. *Vide supra*.

of eighteenth-century philosophy on education was, paradoxically, not in France (where government was too inefficient and chaotic) but in Switzerland, Holland and Prussia. Switzerland was an international focus of ideas; it was prosperous and already had fairly advanced social services. Holland and Prussia, both overrun by the armies of Napoleon, looked to a national system of education to regenerate their people's morale and material condition. The prophetic voice of Rousseau was echoed by Pestalozzi at Zürich and Froebel in Germany.

The English, never very susceptible to philosophical inspiration, and spared the political upheavals that shook the Continent at the end of the eighteenth century, were impelled more prosaically to universal education by the Industrial Revolution. England had the advantage and disadvantage of undergoing industrialization nearly a century ahead of the Continent.

The first effect of industrialization was to make literacy a necessity. An agricultural economy, governed by the sun and the seasons, can work with an illiterate people. But an urban industrial economy, where operations are governed by the clock, requires a minimum of literacy to read notices, instructions, time-tables, temperature- and pressure-gauges.

It cannot be claimed that, in the early years of the movement towards universal education, there was much concern for the individual child as such. The monitorial system, payment by results, and the very large classes in the elementary schools, remind us that the national policy was to inculcate the Three R's into as many children as possible as cheaply as possible. Nevertheless, throughout the nineteenth century in England, the drive towards literacy was powerfully aided by a genuinely humanitarian desire to rescue the children from the factories. And this concern about the fate of the children,[1] together with the increasing provision of schools, prepared the ground for later scientific child-study and the enlightened primary education of our own day.

The modern study of individual children, prophetically heralded by Rousseau, and carried on by Pestalozzi and Froebel, led to the whole child-study movement of the present century, from Sully to Piaget. In modern primary education, which is free from vocational direction, and comparatively free from examinational constriction, the child has come into his own. Good primary schools go a long way towards the realization

---

[1] Cf. the Christian Socialists, F. D. Maurice, Charles Kingsley. 'The great problem of all ... is how to make men know that they are persons, and therefore that freedom and order are their necessary and rightful inheritance.' F. D. Maurice: *Learning and Working*, Lecture IV. Although Maurice was mainly interested in adult education, Charles Kingsley's *Water Babies* did much to arouse the public conscience on behalf of the children.

of John Dewey's ideal of the nurtured growth of the unique individual in community with others.

A significant feature of modern child-study is that the object of study is the individual-in-relation-with-others. The individual is unique, and must be understood and treated as such. But he cannot exist *in vacuo*. The individual grows in community with others, and has obligations to the community as the community has to the individual. The modern study of the learning process is a good illustration. At one time learning might have been thought of in simple terms of individual pupils, each of them at the receiving end of a line from the teacher. Today, learning is known to be a very complex process, into which enter not only the teacher–pupil relation, but all the intricate pupil-interrelations, in the class and in the school, and also the further relations involving home and neighbourhood. At no stage of education is there any escape from the social involvement which is the condition of growth as well as a source of strain and conflict.

If we turn to secondary and higher education, the conflicts in education are more apparent. On the one hand, industrialization, which began by making literacy necessary, has come, with more and more scientific development, to step up the demands on human intelligence, so that the modern industrial society cannot afford to waste any potential skill, and is therefore committed to the provision of maximum educational opportunity for all. In this sense the technological society enhances the educational value of the individual.

On the other hand, our secondary and higher education plentifully illustrate the conflict between the needs of the individual and the claims of society from which education can never escape. Secondary education, for the more intelligent pupils at any rate, is largely shaped by the academic requirements of the institutions of higher education to which they aspire. And, in higher education – especially in technological fields – the dilemma of the modern State is apparent: how far to finance students to follow studies of their own choice, and how far to adjust grants to individuals and institutions in order to attract the required number of trainees in particular fields.

It would be easy to find many more illustrations of conflict, in modern education, between individual and society. It is barely a century since Herbert Spencer expressed his horror at the idea of *compelling* parents to have their children educated. Today, when we accept compulsory education, it is doubtful how much of the parents' choice of school, proclaimed in the 1944 Act, in fact remains. If Comprehensivism prevails in secondary education, variety of schools, and therefore the possibility of choice, will be further diminished. And it is at least debatable whether the egalitarianism of the Comprehensivists should be seen as exalting the individual (by giving every child an equal opportunity) or as drowning the individual in an ocean of uniformity (where it is undemocratic for one child to be more intelligent than another).

Finally, it is worth considering the problem of individual and society within the school community. The most obvious fact is that the school is normally the child's first experience of systematic government, of the rule of law. Family life will already have taught the child the meaning of close personal relations (not invariably agreeable ones); and it is on close personal relations that the value of larger social organizations in the last analysis depends. But family relations are for the most part informal, and it is at school that the child first experiences formal social organizations, with constituted authorities, rules, sanctions, rank and status, rights and duties, and established customs (which can be even more tyrannical than rules).

To a considerable extent the child's later attitudes towards government and citizenship depend on his early response to the school situation. Although (*pace* a few ultra-'progressive' examples) the school cannot be a democracy in the same sense as an adult community can be democratic, there is nevertheless room, in the intelligent and imaginative running of a school, for a great deal of education in citizenship. Pupil-opinion can be consulted, decisions can be explained and discussed. Persons in authority can be approachable. In short, the whole thing can make sense, so that the members of a well-run school, although they will not individually like or approve everything that is done, will on the whole be loyal members of a community that they believe in.

There are bound to be strains and stresses in the school community, as in any society. Broadly speaking, there are two kinds of relation to be considered: relations of pupils with one another, and relations between pupils and teachers. What proportion of pupils *enjoy* school? Most of them probably do not ask themselves the question; they accept school as something that happens. But one could say that the really unfortunate boys and girls are those who do not get on with one another or with the staff. They may be few; but they matter. They feel themselves to be failures, socially, athletically, academically. Those who get on with one another – whether as good athletes or just as good fellows – are usually happy, even if they fall foul of the staff. Those who are academically successful have no fears of the staff; they may, if indiscreetly priggish, be unpopular with their contemporaries, but they will at least have the self-respect that comes from knowing that they are good at *something*.

It is the boy or girl who apparently is not good at *anything* who is likely to be unhappy at school. In the last half-century, however, the range of opportunities has in all schools increased; so that, although there is in a sense no answer to the problem of the boy or girl who is not successful at anything, there is at least a far greater chance than there used to be of the individual finding something that he can do to his own and other people's satisfaction. This enrichment of opportunities not only benefits individuals, but civilizes public opinion. That is to say, it encourages a more liberal recognition of distinction, so that excellence in drama or music may rank with prowess on the football field.

It is impossible to exaggerate the importance of giving each individual the opportunity to do *something* well. As the Newsom Report puts it: 'The less able of our boys and girls are good at so few things that it is surely common sense to let them develop what strengths they have.' A sense of achievement is necessary to self-respect and therefore to the healthy growth of personality. To say this is by no means to deny the Christian virtue of humility. Failure breeds its own unlovely kind of aggressiveness. When Disraeli said: 'Every young man has a right to be conceited until he is successful', he was saying provocatively that success can be truly humbling because it brings glimpses of more remote horizons. In the parable of the Talents, the man who went and buried his one talent may have been discouraged, at the time of distribution, by some such remark as: 'I don't expect we'll get much out of you!'

One of the school's most important functions is to enable boys and girls to discover what is involved in reconciling the needs of the individual with the legitimate claims of society. Something was said in an earlier paragraph about the value of a diversified programme of options, so that boys and girls can find what suits them best; and earlier still, reference was made to the dangers, in our highly organized society, of excessive pressures on the individual. If, during school years, boys and girls can learn in practical experience what it means to belong to a community which makes a sincere effort to realize the principle: Each for all, and all for each, they will have gained something that will remain with them through life, and may help them to make the larger world of adult citizenship better than they found it.

The difficulty of this practical social education arises largely from the fact that the problem of balancing self and community is different for every individual, according to character and temperament. Some people naturally dominate, some are naturally submissive. Some are natural rebels, some natural conformists. Some must be curbed, others encouraged. Somehow or other, any collection of people, if it is to be a community and not a chaos, has to shake down into a workable pattern of inter-relation. As to how that is to be done, one can only say that there are no rules of thumb. The quality of a community is in the last resort the quality of its members. Intelligence, imagination and sympathy are bound to help; stupidity and selfishness are bound to hinder. School life at least offers the opportunity both to practise and to reflect upon social relations, and to experiment within the safety-limits of certain controls.[1]

[1] If the pupil-power movement develops dramatically, this sentence may be out of date before publication.

BIBLIOGRAPHY

BANTOCK, G. H., *Education in an Industrial Society* (Faber and Faber, 1963).
BOTTOMORE, T. B., *Élites and Society* (Penguin, 1966).
BRUBACHER, J. S., *A History of the Problems of Education* (McGraw-Hill, 1947).
BUBER, M., *Between Man and Man* (Collins, Fontana Library, 1961).
COLLIER, K. G., *The Social Purposes of Education* (Routledge and Kegan Paul, 1959; 2nd Impression 1962).
DEWEY, J., *Democracy and Education* (Macmillan, 1916; reprinted 1955).
DOUGLAS, J. W. B., *The Home and the School* (McGibbon and Kee, 1964).
ELVIN, H. L., *Education and Contemporary Society* (C. A. Watts, 1965).
ERIKSON, E. H., *Childhood and Society* (Penguin 1957; reprinted 1965).
FLOUD, J. E., et al., *Social Class and Educational Opportunity* (Heinemann, 1957).
FURNEAUX, W. D., *The Chosen Few* (O.U.P., 1961).
GARFORTH, F. W., *Education and Social Purpose* (Oldbourne Press, 1962).
HALSEY, A. H. (ed.), *Ability and Educational Opportunity* (O.E.C.D., Paris, 1961).
HALSEY, A. H., et al. (eds.), *Education, Economy and Society* (Free Press, Glencoe, 1963).
HUDSON, W. D., (ed.), *The Is/Ought Question* (Macmillan, 1969).
MARITAIN, J., *True Humanism* (G. Bles, 1938).
MEAD, M., *Growing Up in New Guinea* (Penguin, 1942; reprinted 1963).
MEAD, M., *Coming of Age in Samoa* (Penguin, 1943; reprinted 1963).
MUSGRAVE, P. W., *The Sociology of Education* (Methuen, 1965).
OTTAWAY, A. K. C., *Education and Society* (Routledge and Kegan Paul, 2nd Revised Edition 1962).
POPPER, K. R., *The Open Society and Its Enemies* (Routledge and Kegan Paul, 5th Revised Edition 1966).
WISEMAN, S., *Education and Environment* (Manchester University Press, 1964).

Chapter 3
Freedom and Authority

The conflict in human experience, which we have examined in terms of the Individual and Society, reappears in the form of Freedom and Authority.

What do we mean by freedom? In its most elementary form, freedom means the liberty to act according to preference – that is to say, the opportunity to exercise choice.

Before going further, we must ask the question whether, in reality, we have any choice; that is to say, we must look at the problem of determinism and freewill. There is no need to discuss the problem at length, because all reasonable people, even if they *say* they are determinists, *act* as if they had choice. Indeed it is doubtful whether one can act otherwise. We have to concede that we cannot prove determinism to be false. But we can argue that the consequence of believing it is the destruction of most of the meaning in human life. If choice is an illusion, there can be no praise or blame, and no responsibility (but our social, political and legal systems assume that there is).

Moreover, we can say that the problem is not essentially altered by sophisticated presentations which appear to reconcile determinism and choice. For example, we can say that we make choices, but that the choices we make are ultimately and irresistibly conditioned. This is only to move the determining forces a step back. Either an act of choice is something that might have been different, or it isn't. As Sir Isaiah Berlin puts it: 'Men have at all times taken freedom of choice for granted in their ordinary discourse. And ... if men became truly convinced that this belief was mistaken, the revision and transformation of the basic terms and ideas that this realization would call for would be greater and more upsetting than the majority of contemporary determinists seem to realize.'

We shall therefore assume the reality of choice. And having assumed it, we must recognize that choice is an inalienable part of what being human means, and with it goes the right to have a share in governing the community to which we belong. Paternalism, however benevolent, is degrading.

We must also recognize that, for practical purposes, the opportunity to exercise choice must be real and not only theoretical. We are all at liberty to dine at the Ritz – if we have the right money and the right clothes. There would have been no sense in telling a cotton-mill worker of last century that he was at liberty to take his holidays in the south of France. It is true that there is a sense in which a freedom which is denied can be internalized, since no one can restrict our thoughts. Rousseau said: 'There is liberty in dungeons'; and many political prisoners have kept up their own morale, and even shaken the morale of their keepers, by living on the rich stores of their own minds. The Stoic philosophy to a large extent consisted in being captain of one's soul even though one could not be master of one's fate. We also have to recognize that it is not only external limitations that can nullify the opportunity of choice. We may lose or forfeit our liberty simply by not exercising it. Nevertheless, it is fair to say that, for most people in the general life of society, liberty means not only a theoretical possibility of choice but the practical opportunity of acting according to choice.

Having said this, we immediately have to recognize that, in the real world, our range of choice is limited in various ways. The very idea of choice implies limiting circumstances; in an infinite vacuum choice becomes meaningless.

One of my liberties may conflict with another. I should like to go for a walk. But I also like sitting by the fire. I cannot do both. One person's liberty may conflict with another's. I may be at liberty to kill someone I do not like (in the sense that no one is preventing me); but my victim claims a right to live. An employer is at liberty to offer no more than a starvation wage; the employee demands decent standards of living.

Because liberties conflict, because some actions that we might choose are what we call 'bad', because selection is necessary among even 'good' actions, there must be effective controls (by government and public opinion) if a collection of people is to be a community and not a chaos. If the members of the community understand and endorse those controls, so much the better. We here touch on the question of democracy, which is discussed later in this chapter.[1]

So far the argument has been straightforward. We can agree that liberty, in the sense of opportunity to make choices, is something without which a human being cannot be fully human. And we can also agree that social relations (without which the individual could have no life worth the name) require some limitation of the liberty of each in order to maintain the liberties of all.[2] That proposition involves no difficulty in principle, so long as the limitation of liberties is assumed to be minimal.

---

[1] The common law duty of the citizen to assist the police in preventing a breach of the peace reminds us how deeply rooted the democratic idea is in our tradition.

[2] The various forms of the Social Contract theory were ways of stating just that.

The minimal function of government is to prevent the society from disintegrating. We are only stating the obvious conditions of any workable human society.

The difficulties begin when we go on to ask: What controls? How much control? Why these particular controls? What is the business of government and what is not?

There is presumably universal agreement that the maintenance of order and the prevention and treatment of crime are the proper business of government. But there is no consensus as to what actions should be treated as crimes. Murder, assault, burglary are clear cases. But what of sexual offences? The recent changes of the law relating to prostitution and homosexuality are cases in point (in one case the law was tightened, to prevent accosting in the street; in the other case the law was relaxed). Again, there is no agreement as to how far government should concern itself with censorship of literature and entertainment.

This last matter of censorship is a reminder of another difficult problem, namely: which things should be controlled by government and which by public opinion (perhaps channelled through advisory bodies). There is in any case a connection between government and public opinion, inasmuch as no government can, for any length of time, enforce by law something which is intolerable to public opinion, or refuse to give the force of law to something on which public opinion resolutely insists. Also, especially in this country, there is a close interplay of governmental and voluntary agencies, which makes it impossible to maintain any neat distinction between control exerted by law and control exerted by opinion. Law and opinion are intricately involved with one another, as are the activities of statutory and voluntary agencies.

There is a wide range within which government control can vary between the extreme of jeopardizing the health (mental, moral, and physical) of the community, and even its cohesion, by excessive permissiveness, and the opposite extreme of impoverishing the common life by clamping down on deviations. In the ancient world, Athens and Sparta stand as symbols of the two extremes, the one interesting but explosive, the other monolithic and dull. That there always are limits to what government can afford to permit is illustrated by Aristotle's famous remark that the man who cannot accept the conditions of citizenship is either a beast or a god – and, one might add, it is a matter of complete indifference to the State which he is, so long as he is out of the way. The State hangs Christ and criminals side by side.

If we consider government control from the point of view of the *amount* of control, it is convenient to look at the problem historically. In early times the main function of government was the minimal one of keeping order. Much of the political history of Western Europe could be summarized in terms of the long struggle of national governments to master the centrifugal forces of feudalism. Generally speaking, it was not considered the business of governments to provide social services, and only to a limited extent to control the conditions of manufacture and trade.[1]

It was in the eighteenth century that *laissez faire* (government non-interference in economic affairs) was propounded and became orthodox doctrine. G. M. Trevelyan reminds us that, as so often happens, fact came before theory. The machinery of government in eighteenth-century England was hopelessly out of date and quite incapable of coping with contemporary conditions. The theory of *laissez faire* gave doctrinal respectability to what was happening; and the influential classes of society certainly did not want government interference.

A fact of the greatest importance in English history is that, at the very time when the orthodox doctrine was *laissez faire*, the Industrial Revolution was creating conditions which necessitated government control of economic relations, especially labour-conditions. It is one of the ironies of history that the liberals who passed the first Reform Bill in 1832 expected it to lead to reduced taxation and less State interference, whereas in fact it was the first irrevocable step in the chain of events leading to the modern Welfare State.

The past hundred years have seen, in the 'democratic' countries, an enormous increase in government activity, nominally in the interests of, and with the support of, an ever-widening electorate. Even more recently the spread of Communism has created, over half the world, governments which (by democratic standards) reverse the priorities as between individual liberty and State control. To put it crudely, both democracy and Communism ask the citizen to accept more and more government control, and both offer the carrot of an eventual expansion of opportunities for individual self-fulfilment. The difference is that democracy invites the

[1] This is of course a generalization. Throughout the later Middle Ages in Britain the national government tried, with varying degrees of success, to encourage or discourage certain trades by means of tariffs and price-fixing, and to control rates of interest. After the Black Death (in the mid-fourteenth century) the government tried in vain, by Statutes of Labourers, to keep agricultural wages from rising. Attempts to control the balance of foreign trade (Mercantile Theory) went on into the eighteenth century. Apprenticeship in the Middle Ages was controlled by the guilds and municipalities; Elizabeth's Statute of Apprentices (1563) was the first attempt by the central government to control it. Tudor governments tried, with little success, to control the enclosure of land. The dissolution of the monasteries (in the mid-sixteenth century) led to attempts to deal with unemployment, consolidated in the Elizabethan Poor Law – though these early attempts at social legislation scarcely accord with our notions of a Welfare State.

citizen to exercise responsible choice all along the line (by choosing representatives and policies), while Communism invites the citizen to accept in faith the dictates of the Party, believing that in the end it will turn out for the best. A comparable difference of emphasis is observable if we compare the Protestant and Catholic wings of the Christian Church.

In both forms of government there has been, during the present century, a very great increase in the pressures, upon the citizen, of a technocratic and bureaucratic civilization. We are perhaps not over-sensitive to these pressures so long as the machinery works. There is something to be said for a world in which we live by pressing buttons, and do not have to pay school bills and doctors' bills. It is when the machinery breaks down that we experience helplessness and frustration – when the telephone goes wrong, or many hundreds of square miles are plunged into darkness because of one great power failure; when the queues in the doctor's surgery grow longer and longer and the doctor's temper grows shorter and shorter; when one finds oneself tangled up in related social services in such a way that Service *A* cannot move until one has got clearance from Services *B* and *C*, and *C* can do nothing until one has cleared one's position with *A*.

The result of all this is a great increase of tension between liberty and authority which provokes people to react against it. Under a totalitarian form of government there may be insurrections (as in the satellite countries), there may be an underground of criticism and satire, and individuals may try to escape across the frontiers. In the democracies there is more elbow-room for overt discontent, which may show itself in more or less organized campaigns of protest, and in the phenomenon of the social drop-out. The hippie movement can reasonably be regarded as a protest against the technocratic society, constructing an 'anti-system' to contradict the Establishment.[1]

So far we have been discussing freedom in its primary sense of liberty to act according to choice, and authority in its complementary sense of the control necessary to contain the centrifugal forces of individual choice. In these senses, liberty and authority are the twin poles about which any human society must revolve.

Since the need for government itself arises from the fact of human imperfection, there can be no tidy theoretical answer to the question what should be permitted, forbidden, or required. In practice the answer depends on weighing up the probable consequences of permitting or forbidding this or that. The over-all consideration is the maintenance of an ordered

---

[1] Cf. Colin Wilson: *The Outsider*, which is a study of the individual who cannot 'belong' in modern society. Also Richard Neville: *Play Power* (Jonathan Cape, 1970), a study of the hippie movement.

society within which individuals and groups may feel reasonably free as well as secure.

The situation can be summarized in these words of Sir Isaiah Berlin's: 'There is a minimum level of opportunity for choice – not of rational or virtuous choice alone – below which human activity ceases to be free in any meaningful sense. It is true that the cry for individual liberty has often disguised desire for privilege, or for power to oppress and exploit, or simply fear of social change. Nevertheless the modern horror of uniformity, conformism, and mechanization of life is not groundless.'[1]

And it is salutary to remember that crimes against the human spirit may be committed, not only by avowed tyrannies, but in the name of democracy, social welfare and the public good. We may yet be suffocated by the Welfare State.

We have not done with the problem of freedom by discussing it only in terms of liberty to act according to preference, irrespective of what objects are preferred. It is true that, in Sir Isaiah Berlin's words quoted above, 'there is a minimum level of opportunity for choice – *not of rational or virtuous choice alone* – below which human activity ceases to be free in any meaningful sense'. In other words, if we cannot make wrong choices, we cannot in any real sense choose at all, but are like bees and ants, driven by their instinctive urges to perform their various functions in the complex community.

Nevertheless, we must consider not only the liberty of the individual to do as he chooses, but what kinds of things he chooses to do. Some activities are self-fulfilling; some are self-frustrating. Some are helpful to other people; some are socially harmful. This distinction between good and bad choices cannot be denied in principle, although there can be much argument about particular cases (e.g. whether the use of a certain drug is beneficial or harmful).

By taking account of the objects of choice we have given another dimension to the meaning of freedom. We can say that a man is free in proportion as his choices contribute to his fuller growth as a rational and responsible person, and that he is unfree in proportion as his choices have the opposite effect of stultifying his faculties or ruining his health.

Moreover, the use of the terms 'rational' and 'responsible' means that the choice must be the man's own. He is not free if he is being pushed, though it be in the right direction. He must go of his own accord, knowing why and where he is going. At this level, personal responsibility is all-important.

A man's responsibility for making the best of himself must include his

[1] Introduction to *Four Essays on Liberty*, p. lii.

relations with other people – what he can give to them and what he can receive from them: in other words, his duty towards his neighbours, considered both as individuals with whom he has dealings and as a community whose *ethos* largely conditions his opportunities. We can therefore ask, not only whether a man is free (in the sense that he chooses the things that fulfil him as a person), but also whether a community is free (in the sense that it provides maximum conditions for its members to achieve personal freedom). The *ethos* of a community is a very important thing, especially in the case of smaller and more intimate communities, where attitudes are formed which may be transferred to wider fields.[1]

Freedom, in the deeper sense which we are now considering, thus includes self-limitation, or self-discipline, in the interests of others as well as of oneself. It is worth noting in passing that everything a man does, everything indeed that a man *is*, is liable directly or indirectly to affect others. John Stuart Mill's convenient distinction between acts which affect others and acts which affect only oneself is unfortunately false. It would follow from Mill's distinction that a man should not be drunk in the street, but what he does in the privacy of his own rooms is nobody's business. The truth is that everything we do affects us as persons, changes us however slightly, and thereby changes the impression we make on others. One of the things we have to learn through life is that there is nothing – no act or word or thought – that 'doesn't count'. 'It meant nothing at all'; 'I've put all that behind me'; these phrases and others like them may certainly have a legitimate meaning, but not quite the meaning they are supposed to have when offered as desperate excuses.

The freedom that we are discussing has to be achieved by the person for himself. It cannot be manufactured for him. Rousseau's words, 'Freedom is obedience to a law which we prescribe to ourselves' are a reminder that the free man endorses the law by which he lives, makes that law his own. In this connection it is illuminating to study St Paul's progress through 'bondage to the Law' to freedom. Paul in bondage to the Law was the man reluctantly, and not always successfully, doing his irksome duty. 'The good that I would I do not, and the evil that I would not, that I do.' At this stage of his spiritual journey, Paul was in bondage in a double sense – partly because the Law takes away the liberty to do as one pleases, and partly because the Law, while laying down what a man should do, does not give him the power to do it. St Paul, after his conversion, became free, paradoxically by becoming the servant (strictly 'slave') of Christ. His new freedom had the warmth and enthusiasm of a personal relation, so that no material sufferings and calamities were of any account

[1] The *ethos* of the school community is discussed later.

in comparison. He also shared in the power and authority which, in his Master, had its source in perfect identification with the will of his Father.[1]

It is time to see what, in terms of this deeper meaning of freedom, has happened to the concept of authority. When we were considering freedom in its elementary sense of liberty to act according to preference, authority (whether of law or opinion) appeared as an external controlling force. Liberty and authority thus appeared in opposition to one another. In the deeper sense of freedom, however, authority is internalized. At this level, the only satisfactory authority must be (to use an old-fashioned term) the authority of conscience. Freedom and authority have become one and the same thing. If the mature person accepts the law of the land, he accepts it because he believes that, generally speaking, it is right; he does not believe it to be right *because* it is the law. He is unlikely to approve of the law in every particular. And he may disapprove to such an extent that he is bound to consider whether, on balance, he can honestly go on being a citizen of that State. But before coming to desperate conclusions, he will use whatever means are available for trying to get the law changed.

The mature man is the free author of what he must do. If at first sight this proposition appears self-contradictory, perhaps a little reflection will illuminate it. It was Karl Marx who said: 'Freedom is the recognition of necessity' – though the historical necessity that Marx had in mind was something very different from the inner spiritual necessity that claimed St Paul on the Damascus road. But we can see the oneness of freedom and necessity in high moral decision (Luther: 'Ich kann nicht anders'), in great art (when the artist cannot say whether he is the master or the inspired slave of his art), and in the prophetic word ('The word of the Lord came unto X the prophet ...'). In all great creative effort there is a vision of the goal of endeavour which both commands and liberates – liberates *for* the fulfilment of the enterprise, and *from* all compromising distractions and fears.

One of the things we have to learn is that permissiveness is not liberating. It is discipline that liberates. The disciplined musician or painter is the free artist, because only the disciplined artist can perform to his own or other people's satisfaction. The disciplined life is the free life. The disciplined man is the free man.

Few of us can attain to this kind of maturity. But most of us travel far enough on the way towards it to catch at least a glimpse of what it means. Meanwhile, in the imperfect world of practical experience, we need a scaffolding of law and opinion to govern the behaviour of the

[1] See a fuller discussion of St Paul's freedom in Chapter 4 of my *Truth is not Neutral*.

immature of all ages. This is 'authority' in its elementary sense, corresponding with the elementary sense of freedom as liberty to act according to preference.

This general discussion of freedom and authority may suitably end with a consideration of democracy, since democracy claims to generate ordered freedom better than other forms of government.

If we are to understand the democratic ideal, we must not confuse it with the inevitable expedients of practical administration. The essence of democracy, as Rousseau clearly saw, does not consist in counting heads. In practice we have to use this rough and ready method of ascertaining what people think and want. But we all know that it is readily open to abuse: that voters can be bought and bullied and cajoled; subjected to all kinds of pressure which falsify the results. A corrupt democracy can be worse than an enlightened dictatorship. Counting heads is not, in itself, democracy. It is only a very rough and ready approximation to the ascertainment of a consensus which, if it exists at all, defies quantification.

There is indeed an inescapable paradox in democracy, in that, to quote Mr Anthony Lejeune,[1] 'to participate ... implies a liability to be bound by decisions of which one disapproves, or, at best, to be represented by opinions with which one disagrees ... True participation was found only in those old-fashioned African tribes where all the tribesmen talked the whole matter out, for days if need be, until they reached an agreed decision. The idea of voting, that the views of the majority should simply and crudely prevail, they regarded, when white men told them about it, as anti-rational and tyrannical. And, of course, they were right. The trouble is that to require unanimity, even from a small committee, let alone from a mass meeting, is, in the conditions of Western society, impracticable.' Mr Lejeune might have referred also to the Quaker practice of quietly awaiting the 'sense of the meeting' – much more truly democratic than majority rule, but an impossible way to run a country or even a town.

The essence of democracy is to be found in Rousseau's idea of the General Will, which is 'general', not because it is the will of all (which it usually is not), but because it seeks the common good. Rousseau recognizes that the will of all is liable to confusion and corruption, and that the General Will may not effectively emerge. Nevertheless, the health of the community depends on the extent to which the General Will is a reality, that is, on the extent to which the members of the community share a common understanding of what the society stands for and a common will to promote it. Rousseau does not claim that a democratic form of

[1] *Daily Telegraph*, June 7, 1969.

government is the only one that can give expression to the General Will, but only that the General Will has a better chance of gaining expression if the citizens take an active part in government.

Rousseau's doctrine is a dangerous one, as history proves. Since the General Will is not to be identified with the will of all, any group or party may claim to embody the General Will. Scarcely had Rousseau's doctrine been delivered to the world than it was seized and turned upside-down by Robespierre and his Reign of Terror. By claiming that his party had a monopoly of the General Will, Robespierre reversed the ideals of 1789. Marxist Communism is the great modern example of the doctrine that a specially enlightened party is entitled to sovereign power because it knows best.

There is no escape from the dangers of Rousseau's doctrine by identifying democracy with majority-rule. In these days of universal education and the mass media, voters doubtless have more information than they had half a century ago. But they are also more vulnerable, both morally and intellectually. More information can mean misinformation. And the arts of persuasion (whether used by advertiser or politician) can undermine integrity. Democracy is certainly not to be identified with counting votes. We may count votes and yet have no more than a sham democracy. Nevertheless, we must use the device of vote-counting for want of a better one, and do our best, through education, to equip citizens to make wise use of their franchise.

From any point of view, democracy is a dangerous adventure, and does not become any less so in the modern world. There is moreover a sense in which democracy is bound to fail, because it attributes to all enfranchised citizens something which most of them have not got: well-informed, reasoned, and responsible judgement. But, just because democracy pays this compliment to common humanity, and by doing so affirms its faith in the ultimate human values, it is not only the best form of government, but perhaps the only form of government which human beings can accept without forfeiting their human dignity.

Not only is democracy dangerous; it is in danger. In the early 1950s the American publicist, Walter Lippmann, wrote the following in the *Herald Tribune*:

'At the beginning of this century the acknowledged model of a new government, even in Russia, was a liberal democracy in the British or the French or the American style. Think what has happened to the western world and to its ideas and ideals during the forty years since the World Wars began. The hopes that men then took for granted are no longer taken for granted. The institutions and the way of life which we have inherited, and which we cherish, have lost their paramount, their almost undisputed, hold upon the allegiance and the affections and the hopes of the peoples of the earth. They are no longer universally accepted as being the right way towards the good life on this earth. They are fiercely challenged abroad; they are widely doubted and they are dangerously violated even here at home.

'During this half century the power of the western democratic nations has been declining. Their influence upon the destiny of the great masses of people has been shrinking. We are the heirs of the proudest tradition of government in the history of mankind. Yet we no longer find ourselves talking now – as we did before the First World War – about the progress of liberal democracy among the awakening multitudes. We are talking now about the defence and the survival of liberal democracy in its contracted area.

'We are living in an age of disorder and upheaval. Though the United States has grown powerful and rich, we know in our hearts that we have become, at the same time, insecure and anxious. Our people enjoy an abundance of material things, such as no large community of men has ever known. But our people are not happy about their position or confident about their future. For we are not sure whether our responsibilities are not greater than our power and our wisdom.'

Walter Lippmann goes on to urge the need for much greater educational effort if democracy is to be saved. He gives figures to show that, during the half-century since 1900, the ratio of educational expenditure to what he calls 'public task' (Federal expenditure, including defence) has fallen from one in two to one in six. We know that statistics are always a hazardous basis for argument. And we know that expenditure on education is no accurate measure of its quality. Yet there is little doubt that, in the Western countries generally, we are not yet taking education seriously enough as a means of conserving and promoting those values which are our most precious possession. It is a great mistake to suppose that the virtues of democracy are self-evident, or that democratic citizenship requires no learning. A reasonable and responsible self-governing community is something that has to be worked for, taught and learnt for, prayed for, and never regarded as something that will automatically carry on under its own momentum.

The 'education of the whole child' has become a catch-phrase of educational theory, owing in no small measure to the teaching of John Dewey, whose published work spans the first half of this century. The phrase means not only that education is concerned with moral and aesthetic as well as with intellectual development, but (as expounded and practised by Dewey) also that the education of personality is achieved, not by instruction merely, but by practical experience of social living, through which the child can gradually learn the freedom of self-discipline.

There is nothing new in the idea that education is concerned with qualities of character as well as with academic instruction. It is as old as Plato, and indeed much older. In the Middle Ages, education promoted by the Church was concerned with the souls as well as the brains of pupils. The two main secular channels of medieval education, chivalry and apprenticeship, were interested in their pupils' personal development as well as in their technical skills.

It is true that the eighteenth century is the time when 'child-centred' education is generally reckoned to have begun – that phrase meaning that the content and methods of education should be dictated by the real needs of the child's nature rather than by adult notions of what the child ought to have. Two main historical influences have combined to give education this modern orientation. One is the Naturalistic movement of the seventeenth and eighteenth centuries, the spirit of which was clearly expressed by Comenius (1592–1670): 'If we wish to find a remedy for the defects of nature, it is in nature herself that we must look for it, since it is certain that art can do nothing unless it imitates nature.' His ideas were developed by Rousseau (1712–78), Pestalozzi (1748–1827), and Froebel (1782–1852). The other main factor, clearly connected with the preceding, is the more modern application (mainly during the present century) of scientific psychology to the study of children.

Although the principle has long been established that education should concern itself (to quote the Act of 1944) with the 'spiritual, moral, mental and physical welfare' of children, there have ironically been two influences that have narrowed the scope of educational endeavour. One was the nineteenth-century drive for literacy on the cheap, which was referred to in Chapter 2, and which has left a lasting mark on our educational system. The Hadow Report of 1926 proclaimed in principle the parity of status of all schools for children over the age of eleven-plus; and the Act of 1944 abolished the term 'elementary' from the official vocabulary, all schooling beyond eleven-plus being henceforth secondary. Yet even today we have not achieved parity of status as between all kinds of secondary school. It is a matter of opinion whether the comprehensive school is the best solution of the problem. But it is at least one of the possible solutions of a problem that has been publicly acknowledged for the best part of fifty years.

The other restrictive influence, also mentioned in the last chapter, is the increasing academic pressure at the secondary level, which in turn is due to the vast increase in human knowledge[1] and the increasing competition

[1] The increase in modern knowledge inevitably breeds more and more specialists, who know less and less what other specialists are doing.

for entry to universities and other branches of higher education. The result of this increased examination pressure is not only to emphasize intellectual training at the expense of broader personal education, but also to diminish the value of that intellectual training by stressing factual knowledge at the expense of original and critical thought.

It is salutary to recognize that our educational practice falls short of our educational ideals. That, however, is no reason for despair, but rather for taking full advantage of the opportunities that school life offers for helping boys and girls to deepen their understanding and experience of freedom and authority – that is to say, to grow as persons.

What can be done within the school community? A first condition is the maintenance of enough control to preserve order, without which nothing else of value can be done. In the government of any community it is a good general rule that control should be minimal. Unnecessary rules are irksome; there is wisdom in the classic, if apocryphal, example of the school which had only one rule: obedience to common sense. At the same time we have to remember that a school is a community of immature people, who, because of their immaturity, need guidance. The fact that young people dislike being told what to do makes the task of guiding them more difficult, but no less necessary.

Secondly, every effort should be made to help boys and girls to understand (and thus to participate intelligently in) the running of the school community. The fruit of good discipline is active co-operation, not merely passive submission. Superficially it might seem that, in these days of teenage rebellion, protest, and pupil-power, there is no danger of passive submission. On the other hand, those who rebel against the Establishment are often servile conformists in their rebel-group; they have only exchanged one kind of submission for another. Nor does rebellion necessarily imply a desire for responsibility. Not so long ago the Headmaster of Cheltenham wrote: 'We should not be misled by the apparent clamour for participation and for the right to run things in the universities and colleges. They do not want to run them, but they do want to criticize. They want to have representation without functional responsibility. ... Schools must above all have the courage to insist that freedom demands service and involvement and is not merely licence to contract out.'[1]

It is the task of education to cultivate the qualities of personally responsible citizenship. This is a difficult task, because it demands of the citizen not only intelligence and courage, but also something which the young find very difficult: the patient suspension of judgement, pending fuller inquiry and further evidence. The impatience of the young – their habit of acting on impulse – makes them difficult to govern. The young cannot

[1] Mr David Ashcroft, *Daily Telegraph*, June 28, 1969.

learn from experience which they have not yet had, however plainly the probable consequences are spelt out.

School life makes very great demands on the teachers, whose service as guides, philosophers and friends is much more important than their work as academic instructors. There can be no more demanding job, mentally and morally, than teaching; and anyone who suggests that teachers have a clean and cushy job, with short hours and fantastically long holidays, is culpably misinformed. Teachers are responsible not only (in the manner of employers) for their pupils' technical competence in specific tasks, but for their pupils as whole persons.[1] They are the chief agents in creating *ethos*, which is admittedly the least definable, though perhaps the most important, quality of a school.

It has been well said that a teacher should be *an* authority, and *in* authority, but should not be authoritarian.[2] In other words, the good teacher's authority derives from his knowledge, experience and wisdom, and not from his status.

Teachers need humour and humanity, sympathy and understanding. They must be able to tolerate trivial (though perhaps irritating) deviations, but to stand firm on things that matter. The young need a dependable moral framework to support and contain them. They also need to experiment. They need both adventure and security – which, after all, are other names for freedom and authority. Even in revolt, they need something to push against; you cannot dive if the diving-board is not there – which is another reminder that permissiveness is not freedom. One of the most valuable experiences for the young is to grow up in the company of older people who know their own minds, have clearly thought-out opinions, and cannot be influenced by fear or other emotional pressures. It matters comparatively little whether boys and girls *accept* the opinions of their elders; almost certainly they will go through a phase of rejecting them. What matters far more is that they should learn, by personal association, what kind of people these are – that they have thought their way through to beliefs which they are prepared to stand by. It is an especial privilege for the young to know at close quarters people who, having come through doubt, confusion and conflict, are free from fear. Fear is the source of petty tyranny as it is of lenience. Fear, not hate, is the real opposite of love. In the long run it is love that casts out fear. We do not often in our lives meet people who are free from fear; but, if in our youth we have known one or two such, we shall have gained something unforgettable.

The education of boys and girls in a sense of responsibility to others

---

[1] This responsibility is of course shared with the parents. More will be said later about the parent–teacher relation.

[2] Professor R. S. Peters.

and to themselves is no easy task. In the glow of physical health, with all the time in the world before them, they feel no need to conserve either health or time. If they are in training for a particular contest, they will train rigorously. Otherwise, whose business is it but their own what they do with their bodies? If a vital examination is imminent, they will burn the midnight oil. Otherwise, why go out of your way to improve your mind? And, in their sense of duty to their neighbour, the young are capricious and paradoxical. Capable of giving themselves generously, they will throw themselves into VSO and other good causes. Yet, again, they are capable of the kind of defiant self-interest illustrated by Fiji Bell, the sleek typist in Philip Oakes's *The God Botherers*: 'I'm only interested in things that affect me.'

One thing in particular that young people need to learn is the difference between toleration and the fellowship (Agapé) which St Paul immortally celebrated in his first Letter to the Corinthians.[1] If any group of people needed that lesson it was the Corinthians, Corinth being perhaps the most permissive society in the Graeco-Roman world. Some of our way-out young people talk a good deal about love and non-violence. What they often mean is something purely negative: a doctrine of live-and-let-live. I can do what I like, and you can do what you like, as long as we don't get in each other's way. There are indeed worse attitudes than this; but it is negative, and is very far removed from the active fellowship of the Christian tradition, the test of which is that a man will go out of his way to help others and will give himself for them. An essential part of growing up is to learn that we grow as persons by giving rather than by getting.[2]

Everything that has been said in this context about teachers and pupils is also true of parents and children. Those children are fortunate whose parents not only are understanding and approachable, but also know their own minds and are not to be driven off course by cajolery, defiance, or other irrelevant pressures. It is often said that the gap between the generations has never been greater than it is today. If this is so, it is partly because the accelerated rate of social change separates the generations more widely than before, partly because the relative affluence of many teenagers gives them a new independence, and partly because, in the confusion of values from which our generation suffers, it is the more difficult for parents to know their own minds about the handling of their children. It has been pointed out[3] that the modern family is a source of stress and

---

[1] 1 Cor. xiii.
[2] See Chapter 2, p. 9.
[3] By Dr Edmund Leach, Provost of King's, Cambridge, in the Reith Lectures for 1967.

strain because it is comparatively small and also comparatively insulated from other families. 'Our present society is very uncomfortable. The parents and children huddled together in their loneliness take too much out of each other. The parents fight; the children rebel.'

It is no easy job to be a parent in these days. And it is no easy job to be a teacher. It is a pity that parents and teachers do not co-operate more effectively in their common task. The jocular suggestion that we would be a better educated society if the children were sent home and the parents brought to school in their place is at least a reminder that we are far from solving the problem of how best to bring together the parents, the teachers and the children. The fact that parent–teacher relations are more effective in some schools than in others suggests that tact, goodwill and persistence can achieve a good deal. There do not appear to be any rules of thumb. Parent–teacher associations flourish in some schools. In some the Head and his staff prefer other methods of enlisting parents' interest. In any case, time and patience are needed; and teachers are already heavily burdened.

In these days when the citizen's function appears to consist largely of queueing at the receiving end of the conveyor-belt of the Welfare State, when education is no longer a coveted privilege to be struggled for, it is not surprising that many parents unthinkingly shunt the responsibility for their offspring on to the school. A mother, criticized for the unruly behaviour of her five-year-old child, said: 'Oh, I know I can't do anything with her. But it doesn't matter. You see, she starts school next week.' A boy of sixteen, asked by a friend how he had got on in an examination, said that none of his family had ever asked him; nor had it occurred to them to ask him any question after his first day at a technical college. It is sometimes suggested that parents who patronize boarding schools are paying to get rid of their children. But, for the very reason that they are paying, and want value for money, these parents often take far more interest in what the school is trying to do for their boys or girls than those whose children go to the secondary modern or comprehensive round the corner.

It is an axiom in the teaching profession that the parent whose intelligent co-operation is most needed is the most difficult to entice within striking distance. But that is no reason for despair. It is a principle of modern military strategy that you go where the going is good. You don't sit down before the impregnable fortress until you starve it into submission. You deploy your forces round it, fighting a war of movement, advancing where you can, and afterwards mopping up behind you. This is clearly the strategy for building good relations between parents and the school. Encourage those who are interested and responsive, build up the right kind of tradition, and hope for a time when the rest will want to get on to the band-waggon.

Taking a still longer view, we must recognize that the problems of the parent–child–teacher relation will not be solved in years but rather in generations. The long-term solution requires that we should become a much better educated nation, which in turn involves the practical application of the principle that education is something that ought to go on throughout life. So long as education is thought of as *terminating* – whether at fifteen or twenty-one – it will not only be incomplete but also pushed out of shape. It is only in proportion as education is thought of as continuing through life that each stage of the process becomes free for its own purpose. Much learning and thinking is more effectively done at the adult stage, as Plato knew well. We may hope that, parallel with the extension of schooling, adult education will also continue to expand, especially in connection with universities (which ought to recognize more fully their responsibility to the general public beyond their walls), local community centres (many of which offer interesting and varied programmes), and radio and television (the vehicles of the Open University).[1]

Education, it has been suggested, should go on throughout life. But we may well ask whether one life is enough – that is to say, in what sense the individual is really the unit of education. It could be argued that, from some points of view at any rate, the family rather than the individual is the educational unit.[2] To say that it takes three generations to produce an educated person would be to overstate the case. Some people are much more readily responsive to cultural influences than others. But the overstatement is at least a reminder of something about education which is often overlooked, especially by egalitarians, namely: the powerful influence of home and neighbourhood on children, especially of pre-school age. By the time the school gets the child, a great deal has already happened to him. We expect the school to produce educated people. Over and above that, we expect the school to exert an educational influence on the parents and homes of the children. To expect miracles of teachers is no doubt to pay them a compliment. But it is hardly realistic. We have to reckon with the fact that, in the normal course of events, and taking into account the many influences (of school, home, neighbourhood, local

---

[1] While the Open University has great possibilities in the field of further and adult education, it is too early to prophesy what success it will have. The unknown factor is the amount of public response, which has been variously estimated at something between 34,000 and 150,000. The expenditure of large sums of money would be worth while only if the number of enrolments were proportionate.

[2] T. S. Eliot said: 'The primary vehicle for the transmission of culture is the family.'

tradition, entertainment media) to which the child is exposed, the work of producing educated people may well spread over several generations, each building on the achievements of the one before.

Discussing the educational thought of T. S. Eliot, Professor G. H. Bantock writes: 'The differences [between people] both manifest and accentuate distinctions in society which our times try hard to cover up. The notion of "classes", ambiguous and ill-defined as it often is, is simply an institutionalized form of these differences. This does not mean that inequalities of ability, sensibility and moral awareness are perfectly reflected in the hierarchy of society; they are not. But the fact of such disparity makes some form of class-structure essential, even if this structure is an imperfect reflection of the inherent inequalities. And these differences are perpetuated by a psychological transmission which reveals an ambiguity in the very notion of education; that the education of family is in most cases more fundamental than formal education, and that therefore, from generation to generation, there takes place a form of transmission that even the all-powerful State cannot *will* out of existence.'[1]

BIBLIOGRAPHY

BANTOCK, G. H., *Freedom and Authority in Education* (Faber and Faber, 1952).
BERLIN, I., *Four Essays on Liberty* (O.U.P., 1969).
CLARKE, F., *Freedom in the Educative Society* (University of London Press, 1948).
CRANSTON, M., *Freedom – A New Analysis* (Longmans, 1955; 2nd Edition, 1967).
DEWEY, J., *Freedom and Culture* (Allen and Unwin, 1940).
JEFFREYS, M. V. C., *Truth is not Neutral* (R.E.P., 1969).
MCCALLISTER, W. J., *The Growth of Freedom in Education* (Constable, 1931).
PETERS, R. S., *Authority, Responsibility and Education* (Allen and Unwin, 1959; 2nd Edition 1963).
PETERS, R. S., *Ethics and Education* (Allen and Unwin, 1966).
POLANYI, M., *The Logic of Liberty: Reflections and Rejoinders* (Routledge and Kegan Paul, 1951).
RADCLIFFE, P. (ed.), *Limits of Liberty* (Wadsworth Pub. Co., Belmont, California, 1966).

[1] G. H. Bantock: *T. S. Eliot and Education* (Faber and Faber, 1970), p. 111.

Chapter 4

Continuity and Change: The Nature of Growth

Reference was made in an earlier chapter to the mystery of personal identity. Each of us is continually changing, physically and mentally; and yet each of us remains himself throughout life. Any change, whether through injury, disease or senility, which is sufficient to cast doubt on a person's continued identity, is recognized as a disorder or abnormality, indicated in such colloquial expressions as 'He is not himself'.

This ever-changing, but continuous, identity is what we call 'growth', and it is the character of all living things. Not only does growth involve a mysterious relation between identity and change; it also involves an equally paradoxical relation between the organism and its environment. All living things are parasitic in the sense that they feed on the environment, taking it into themselves physically and mentally (in those cases where 'mentally' is an appropriate term), assimilating what they need, and rejecting what they do not need. The most intimate relations are between living things of the same kind; but the whole connection of an organism with its environment extends without assignable limit.

There is another feature of growth that should be noticed, namely: coherence, which is really another aspect of continuity or identity. It is of the nature of an organism to grow. And an organism has coherence. The use of the word 'coherence' reminds us that the growing organism not only has continuing identity, in the sense that it is itself and not another organism, but also that it has unity. There may be multiplicity within the unity; that too is characteristic of organisms. But a multiplicity which is not held together in unity is not an organism. An organism must function as *one*. If something happens to break this unity – if, for example, a disease of the cerebellum destroys the power to co-ordinate movements – we would say that growth is interrupted. At the mental level, too, the growing organism must have coherence and consistency of ideas and feelings and impulses. Not that any of us are perfectly coherent. But we must be at least reasonably coherent if we are to be regarded as sane. A person who is mentally disorganized beyond a certain point is mad – and, if he can be said to be growing at all, the growth is at least not healthy.

The mysterious nature of growth is apparent if we ask where the mainspring of growth is located. To put it crudely, is growth something that the organism does, or something that happens to it? Is the entire potential of the organism contained in the seed or the foetus? Can we say, with Froebel, 'All the child is ever to be and to become lies, however slightly indicated, in the child and can be attained only from within outwards'? Or is growth a product of the environment; so that we could say, with Helvétius: *'L'Education peut tout'*?

The truth, of course, is in neither of these extremes. Growth is the *response* of the organism to its environment. There is a given nature, or potentiality. A birch tree may be a success or failure as a birch tree, according to conditions of light, soil, and elbow-room. But it can only be a birch tree; it cannot turn into an oak tree, either because it wants to, or because the environment compels it. To that extent, the organism's potentiality is within it, a *datum*; and the sensible birch tree will try to be the best possible birch tree, and not be led astray by envy of the oak's longevity and prestige into trying to change its nature.

When one says that the individual's identity is 'given', the term is used precisely. However strongly I may feel that I am I, an active, choosing, willing self, responsible for what I am and for what I am becoming, I have to recognize that I did not create myself. There was a time when I was not. Or was there? There is a continuity of substance, and perhaps in some sense of consciousness, in the transmission of being from parents to children. In the last analysis, how distinct is the individual from other individuals?

We also have to recognize that we may exaggerate our day-to-day independence as individuals. Not only do we *like* to think we are captains of our souls, but we are much more easily *aware* of our conscious acts of choice than we are of the subtle influences of people and things upon us. One of the best ways of persuading someone to do something is to get him to believe that it was his own idea.

In recent times the social psychologists and sociologists have done a great deal to bring home to us the salutary knowledge that we are less independent in our thoughts and actions than we usually imagine. Much work has been done, especially in America, on the social factors contributing to the formation of attitudes.[1]

Nevertheless, in the last analysis, the individual's uniqueness is irreducible. No amount of social psychology, and no amount of social pressure, can alter the fact that John Smith is John Smith and not William Jones.

---

[1] The work of Sherif and Cantril is an example. G. W. Allport says: 'The concept of attitude is probably the most distinctive and indispensable concept in contemporary American social psychology.'

Not only is personal uniqueness factually irreducible; it remains a goal on which we set value. The purpose of living is to become more and more ourselves, more fully differentiated. We admire those who are 'personalities', 'characters'; not those who are 'dim' or 'colourless'.

Paradoxically, it is through social intercourse with other people that we become more and more ourselves. The goal of living would seem to be individuality in community. Social intercourse can enrich us as individuals. This enrichment is not automatic. If we allow ourselves to play a merely passive role in company with others, we shall become increasingly sheep-like. But we all know that the creative community is one in which highly developed individuals strike sparks off one another, and where friendship thrives on tension. The healthiest community is the one that can contain the most tension without disintegrating.[1]

This two-way character of personal relations is very apparent in marriage. In a sense each partner would like the other to mirror him- or her-self. Differences of opinion can be painful. 'The twain shall be one flesh.' On the other hand, the whole value of the partnership depends on the 'twain' remaining two people, with minds and bodies of their own. Your wife is no help if she only echoes your own thoughts. If married people are wise, they will respect each other's reasonable freedom and privacy. Nothing is more destructive of happy marriage than over-possessiveness. It is easier to forgive and forget infidelity. Marriage is a profound example of the inner mystery of growth.

It is not only individuals who grow. Communities also grow; and their growth is called history. The essential character of growth – the combination of change and continuity – is seen in history. If there were no change, civilization would silt up like the Sphinx, or at best go round and round in everlasting monotony like an ants' nest. If there were no continuity, change would not be change at all, but the meaningless substitution of one thing for another. The essence of history is that it is significant change. Coherence, which was noted as a feature of the growing organism, is also a feature of a healthy community. There may be many and varied groups within the community. But if it is to be regarded, for example, as a nation, it must have an over-all unity of government and administration, customs and attitudes. Communities, like individuals, can disintegrate.

We must, however, notice a difference between man and the other animals. Social animals have a life-cycle, and the species may change its form and habits in the long process of biological evolution. But neither

---

[1] Politically the extremes are the monolithic one-party State, and the unstable, multi-party State where there is a revolution twice a year. Pericles, in his Funeral Speech, claimed that Athens represented the optimum balance of variety in unity.

of these is what we mean by history. A community can have history only if it can reflect upon its experience, draw inferences from its reflections, and change its behaviour in the light of those reflections. Man alone can do that, so far as we know. Under pressure of circumstances (hunting or food-shortage, for example) animals may within certain limits change their habits. But, in the short term, animal behaviour provides no evidence of the sort of adaptability and adaptation that we recognize as history.

Through its history a community grows, much as an individual grows. It may grow successfully or unsuccessfully, healthily or unhealthily. It may become sick. It can die. Just as the individual's growth depends largely on his relations with others, so does the growth of a community depend on its relations with other communities.

A. J. Toynbee, in his monumental *Study of History*, propounded the theory that a civilization responds to the challenge of difficulty. If life is too easy, and no effort is called for, no advanced civilization is likely to arise. If there is too much difficulty, the civilization will collapse and disintegrate under the burden. The successful civilizations are those which have encountered, and responded to, the optimum amount of difficulty. In the relations between communities, we can see how Toynbee's principle works. One community may be isolated, and, having no stimulus to respond to, stagnates. Another may be exploited, conquered, annihilated. Between the extremes are those contacts between communities by which the commerce, arts and sciences of both are stimulated.

The same law applies to individuals. We know how a child can be discouraged by the challenge of tasks beyond his powers, or can become lazy because he is not being challenged enough. Those who remember the trade depression of the 1930s can recall how prolonged unemployment undermined the morale and prestige of the men who suffered. By contrast, we may think that the modern Welfare State, by making life too easy, is at least one cause of irresponsibility in the young.

If we are right in seeing growth as a character of communities as well as of individuals, then it is as necessary to study the history of a community as it is to study the development of an individual. If an individual presents problems, we seek to know how those problems arose. Equally, we cannot hope to understand the problems of a community – political, economic, cultural – without studying them in their developmental context.

There is indeed no more valuable instrument of understanding than a well-trained historical sense. It is a pity that history is not more taught, and better taught, in our schools. The fact that a boy can stay at school until eighteen, and study no history after the age of fourteen or fifteen, makes no sense in a society that seeks to be an educated democracy.

Some understanding of history is all the more important in a world which is rapidly changing. The spread of political democracy lays heavier obligations on the ordinary man and woman. The increasing interdependence of remote parts of the world makes it more difficult, but also more important, to understand the how and why of particular situations. The growth of science and technology presents us with new possibilities and new risks.

In the progress of civilization, there emerge pastoral, agricultural, industrial and technological societies. Each stage is more complex than the one before, more hazardous in the event of breakdown. The really frightening thing about our technocratic civilization is that, when the machinery goes wrong, not only can we ordinary people do nothing about it; we cannot even understand what is wrong. In the old days, when the horse went lame, or the lamp ran out of oil, we could at least understand what was wrong; and there was a reasonable chance that we could do something about it.

If man is to remain master of his own inventions, and not become their slave – or, worse, be demented by them – he must be able to *understand*. That is why our helplessness is one of the most disturbing features of the technocratic civilization. Not long ago the BBC filmed some interviews with residents on a caravan site which had been without electricity for some days. Without exception the people interviewed confessed their helplessness. 'The washing-machine doesn't work; so I can't do my washing.' 'The spin-dryer won't work.' 'The electric iron won't work.' And, above all, 'The telly doesn't work. So there's nothing to do in the evenings.' Because the current was switched off, the life of a community was switched off. What would these people do if they were spirited back to the days when there were no radios, no spin-dryers or washing-machines, no electricity?

Another disturbing feature of the technocratic civilization which has received a good deal of well-deserved publicity of late is the pollution of the environment, due largely to unforeseen consequences of inventions that appear *prima facie* to be blessings. We have a growing apprehension that the experts may not have as complete a mastery as we supposed.

It is not suggested that historical study can fully equip us to cope with the problems of the technological age. We also need to know a good deal more about the sciences than most of us know at present. Or at least we need to know what is the function and scope of the various sciences: what sort of questions they ask and what sort of answers they are equipped to give – what, in fact, are their terms of reference.

It is, however, worth pointing out that a study of our technological age in the perspective of its development is indeed a historical study. It is that developmental perspective that we need, as an informed habit of mind. It can give us wisdom and the power to suspend judgement. It makes us cautious towards novel invention, and on the look-out for the shocks and disappointments that are so often the backlash of progress. And it will keep us reminded of those abiding problems of man's struggle with his environment through the centuries – problems that have their source, not in techniques, but in the nature of man. In those ways a historical sense can help us to cope with our bewildering world. In the words of R. G. Collingwood: 'What is history for? ... My answer is that history is "for" human self-knowledge ... The value of history ... is that it teaches us what man has done and thus what man is.'

It remains to consider the bearing of this discussion of growth on the problems of education. In modern times, and especially during the present century, there has been much study of the growth of children, both as individuals and in relation to one another. It is also profitable to study the growth of the school community, and the historical development of the educational system. It must, of course, be acknowledged that, when we speak of the 'growth' of a community or institution, we are using the word in a figurative sense. Communities are not in fact organisms; still less are institutions. Yet, if there is any validity in what has been said earlier in this chapter, communities and institutions manifest, in the course of their development, enough of the qualities of organic growth to make the figure of speech illuminating rather than confusing.[1]

A convenient vantage-point from which to see the importance of child-study in modern education is John Dewey's doctrine that Education is Growth. In his *Democracy and Education* he says: 'Since there is nothing to which growth is relative save more growth, there is nothing to which education is subordinate save more education. ... The educational process has no end beyond itself; it is its own end.'

No authority on education has gone further than Dewey in identifying education with growth. It is true that the Naturalistic school of Rousseau, Pestalozzi and Froebel thought of the aims of education in terms of the development of the child's nature and capacities. Froebel, as we saw earlier in this chapter, went so far as to say that *everything* that the child was capable of becoming lay, at least potentially, in the child. It is also true that, centuries before Rousseau, St Thomas Aquinas thought of the

---

[1] We must, however, be on our guard against the dangers of applying the metaphor of organism to an institution such as the State. It suits the apostles of totalitarian government, following Hegel's mystical apotheosis of the State, to ascribe to the State a life and authority, distinct from and above the lives of the citizens. As long as we remember that the community has no existence apart from its members, the metaphor of organism is useful.

child as essentially active and growing; and that, before him, Aristotle and Plato had thought of education in terms of activity and growth.

There was, however, a new element in Dewey's thinking, which earned it the label 'Pragmatism'. Dewey was much influenced by the work of Darwin, whose *Origin of Species* was published in the year of Dewey's birth (1859), and *The Descent of Man* in 1871. Darwin's theory of biological evolution differed from that of his eighteenth-century predecessor, Lamarck, in that Darwin attributed the evolution of species to the natural selection of small chance variations, enabling those individuals to survive which were best adapted to their environment. Evolution was therefore essentially adaptation to situations, and there was no end or purpose in it beyond adaptation itself.[1] For Dewey, growth and education were their own ends. His philosophy was 'pragmatic' in the sense that the question to be asked is: Does it work? The test of growth was that it should lead to more growth, not to some preconceived final goal.

The idea of growth as adaptation led Dewey to emphasize the social aspect of education; education must happen in community. The idea of growth as its own end led him to emphasize the importance of meeting the child's needs *now*, as distinct from trying to prepare him for a future which as yet means little to him. The latter principle was well expressed by Sir John Adams: 'The better the child is as a child; that is, the truer he is to his child nature as such, the better man will he make when the proper time comes.'

These two emphases in Dewey's thought have been very important in modern educational theory and practice. Education in this century probably owes as much to John Dewey as to any other single individual. To acknowledge our practical debt to John Dewey is not, however, to accept his philosophy without criticism. Attractive as the doctrine of growth for growth's sake may be, because it relieves us of the burden of ultimate values and authorities, the fact that growth can be good or bad, healthy or unhealthy, is bound to reassert itself, and with it the question by what criteria we can distinguish right from wrong growth. We find ourselves back again with Aquinas and Augustine, Aristotle and Plato. There must be an end or aim of growth (call it Truth, or Reason, or the Will of God) which is distinguishable from the process of growth itself.

The philosophical dilemma is somewhat similar to that of pure, Benthamite Utilitarianism, in which the criteria of conduct were pleasure and pain. 'Quantity of pleasure being equal, push-penny is as good as poetry.' John Stuart Mill, though nominally a utilitarian, allowed that there were

---

[1] Bernard Shaw says somewhere that, according to Darwin, the giraffe grew a long neck because only the longer-necked ones survived, while, according to Lamarck, the giraffe grew a long neck because it wanted to.

qualities of pleasure as well as quantities, and thus really surrendered the whole position. It is noteworthy that John Dewey not only rebuked those of his disciples who reduced his teaching to a doctrine of uninhibited self-expression, but went some way towards compromising the relativism of his philosophy by proclaiming the need for idealism and intelligent foresight.

The need for aims that will enable us to distinguish right from wrong growth is clear when we consider the dilemma in which Rousseau found himself. If, as he postulated, man is naturally good, and if education is the natural growth of the child, why is human society corrupt and 'man everywhere in chains'? And why do we have to separate the child (as Emile was separated) from the normal environment in order to educate him? The puzzle for the Naturalist school is: If Nature is good why has human nature gone so wrong and human society become so bad?

The history of human thought suggests that man will always recognize the need for ultimate values which are timeless in the sense that they provide standards by which changes of manners, customs, beliefs, can be judged, and in the light of which the future can be planned. Which is only to say that, if man is to go anywhere in an intelligent and responsible way, he must have some idea where he is going. In terms of education, the teacher cannot escape the responsibility of guiding the child's growth, any more than he can escape the fact that it is the child himself who does the growing. Half a century before Dewey, Froebel had given classic expression to this two-sided truth in his image of the school as *Kindergarten* and the teacher as gardener. The gardener plans the arrangement and nurtures the growth of the plants, but he cannot do their growing for them. They alone have in themselves the secret and power of growth. But the gardener can make the difference between a garden and a wilderness.

Modern child-study is associated with such names as Maria Montessori, Arnold and Beatrice Gesell, Charlotte Bühler, Susan Isaacs, and Anna Freud. The most eminent worker in this field is undoubtedly Jean Piaget, who has been publishing his results since 1923. The fact that Piaget's work has roused much controversy, and that he has his critics, is a measure of his importance. Nor have his views remained static through the years. This is not the place for a detailed discussion of Piaget's theories of child development. Any attempt to analyse a continuous process of growth into stages that can be distinguished and labelled is bound to incur the charge of arbitrariness, and is equally bound to differ from some other psychologists' interpretations. On the other hand, it is only by systematizing the raw material that a study can become manageable. In general, the psychologists who have studied the mental growth of children agree that there is a development from a self-centred stage to one of social interaction, and from fantasy to an appreciation of realities, that the child's social and cultural environment is of great importance to his growth, and that learning is most efficient when its materials and methods fit in with the child's stage of development (hence the emphasis on 'readiness').

If we turn our attention to our system of education (its organization, content and method) we see that its development has been slow and distorted. The true nature and purpose of education have been known for 2,500 years or more; and we are still a long way from putting our ideals into practice. That is perhaps not surprising when we observe the imperfections of our civilization after so many millennia of recorded experience, and when we reflect that a system of education is unlikely to be better than the civilization that produced it. Our world is scarcely a garden, for children or anyone else. In this age of unparalleled technological power we go in fear of the political and/or chemical destruction of our civilization.

One of the lessons of history is that good ideas are seldom put into practice simply because they are good ideas. Historical events are produced for the most part by other events. Education has been both promoted and impeded by events that had nothing directly to do with educational thought. It was the growth of trade in the sixteenth and seventeenth centuries that created the demand for increased production and brought about the Industrial Revolution. It was the need for a basically literate proletariat to operate industrial production that promoted the drive for literacy in the nineteenth century. Later on, the need for more highly trained staff for technical and administrative jobs promoted the great expansion of secondary education of which the monument is the Act of 1902. Meanwhile the extension of the franchise made it increasingly apparent that mere literacy was not enough. Democracy needs not only a literate people but an educated people. The result has been the attempt to improve the quality of education for all children over the age of eleven (an attempt advocated in the Hadow Report of 1926 and proclaimed in the Act of 1944). Since it is very much more difficult to educate people than to teach them the Three R's, it is not surprising that we are still floundering in the problems of secondary education.

It would be a useful exercise to draw up a balance-sheet of historical influences for and against our educational development. On the debit side would appear two important factors that were mentioned in Chapter 3. One of these was the attempt to keep down the cost of elementary education in the nineteenth century – partly because the idea of spending public money on education was a new and strange one anyway; and partly because there was some genuine fear among the ruling classes lest too much education might make the lower orders troublesome rather than useful.[1] The other debit factor is the examinations rat-race, which is largely the result of the insatiable demand of an increasingly technological society for highly trained personnel. Secondary, further, and even higher education have to think less of the personal education of the students than of getting them over the academic hurdles. To these influences impeding the real progress of education we might add the confusion of thought about the organization of secondary education produced by the invasion of education by egalitarian political motives. There are some purely educational arguments for the comprehensive school, which deserve consideration. But the educational arguments have been so mixed up with political arguments that the whole issue is befogged. Less than five years ago Sir Alec Clegg, Chief Education Officer for the West Riding and himself a distinguished advocate of comprehensive schools, made some very damaging comments on a scheme for Liverpool, which he described as 'the deplorable business of agglomerating a group of widely separated buildings and calling them a comprehensive school'. Since then, the controversy has become hotter, but no more luminous; and, in spite of government pressure, there is little evidence that local authorities are any more in favour of thorough-going comprehensivism than they were.

Educational progress has been not only slow but complicated in its circumstances. During the past century and more it has involved two emotive issues, social class and religion. Those issues are with us still. It is instructive to study, for example, the fierce and prolonged battle which W. E. Forster had to fight to get the Bill of 1870 through Parliament. Maimed as it was in the course of debate, the Act of 1870 was the first big step towards a national system of education for this country. In the perspective of history there is no doubt that it was a notable achievement, and that Forster did the best possible in the circumstances. But it roused so much controversy that the Liberal Party was split, and lost the general election four years later. Ironically it was a Conservative government in 1876 that began the gradual process of making elementary education compulsory and free, which eventually completed the change to which Forster's Act had in principle committed the country.[2]

---

[1] It is a pity that we cannot have the comments of some of the statesmen of a hundred years ago on the present chaos in the trade union world, and the embarrassment thereby caused to governments of both left and right.

[2] See T. Wemyss Reid: *The Life of the Rt Hon. W. E. Forster*, originally published 1888, republished 1970, Adams and Dart.

It is not surprising that there has been more real progress at the primary level than elsewhere in the system. It is in the primary school, and especially in the infant school, that teachers are free to educate without the pressures that distort the education of older children. And the immediate and obvious bearing of most modern child-study is upon the primary school. Primary education therefore enjoys most inspiration and most opportunity, though perhaps not its fair share of public money. A time may come when teachers in secondary and higher education – even in universities – will take a look at what happens in primary schools, and begin to wonder whether they, in their own work, have anything to learn therefrom. If university and college students are intellectually mature, but irresponsible in their general behaviour, may there not be some imbalance in their education?

The present century has been a time of unprecedented educational effort and educational change. Yet, if we ask what is new in twentieth-century education (apart from the enormous increase of public expenditure upon it), the answer is not so much a new vision of the aims of education as a new armoury of techniques for implementing our aims. These include the systematic child-study to which reference has already been made. There is also the whole range of 'hardware' (largely electronic) which, wisely used, can release the teacher from the old chalk-and-talk routine for more imaginative activity. There are exciting possibilities in the new techniques. But, if we are wise, we shall beware of the dangers of the machine as well as its possibilities. The trouble about mechanizing any process, whether it be making shoes or marking examination papers, is that the machine tends to reduce the operation to what the machine can do. In the marking of examination papers, the machine has the merit of speed, tirelessness, and complete objectivity; it cannot, as yet, evaluate imponderables such as literary style or critical insight. If a time should ever come when a computer could do everything that a human being can do, there would be no point in continuing to breed human beings, nor for that matter in having computers.

A school, like any other community, grows: that is to say, it makes its own history. It is worth looking at some of the problems connected with the changing life of the school. Some of these were noticed in Chapter 3: in particular the relations between teachers and pupils in an age when the gap between the generations is greater, probably, than it has ever been, and adolescents are more precocious than they have been for at least some centuries; and the relations between the parents and the school.

This chapter has been concerned especially with the interplay of continuity and change. In the course of school life children can learn a good

Continuity and Change | 53

deal about growth. As individuals they change greatly during their few years at the school; each boy or girl must, on leaving, look back to that remote day when the threshold was first crossed. They see the others change. And their friendships and enmities change. They see the school itself change, with changes of staff or changes in the character of the neighbourhood. They may think the school has gone down, or that they have done a little to make it better. They may, as prefects, have had opportunity to take responsibility and play some part in the running of the school.

It is a truism never to be forgotten that children like routine. They love tradition. Left to themselves they are more rigid traditionalists than any grown-ups.[1] Tradition and routine are valuable fly-wheels in the social machine, providing useful momentum to carry over rough places. Routine gives a sense of security; and children need security. Wise teachers will not change established customs without very good reason. A new teacher is well advised to follow in his predecessor's footsteps, at least until he has had time to look round. The young are allergic to new-brooming.

On the other hand, the school community must not be too static. There is a difference between stability and death. There must be enough new enterprise (whether curricular or extra-curricular) to rouse interest and provide outlets for initiative.[2]

There are no rules of thumb to govern the balance between continuity and change in the life of a school. In general, there is no point in change merely for the sake of change, for it will appear insincere. Occasionally there erupts into the life of a school a personality of such energy and originality that the school is revolutionized. When F. W. Sanderson went as headmaster to Oundle, it took him some ten years of struggle to convert boys and masters to his ideals; but from then on he had, with few exceptions, their devoted discipleship and, what is more important, there was a rare excitement and enthusiasm in the life and work of the school. Revolutions of this kind cannot be manufactured. But, when they happen, the authority of the past is destroyed and a new world created. In course of time that new world will in its turn become a tradition, which it is impious to question and sinful to change.

One final comment on the subject of education and growth. If education is learning to live, then we have never ceased learning so long as we

---

[1] In the present writer's schooldays it was customary for each successive Head of a House to write out the House rules and post them on the notice-board. But they must be copied exactly from their predecessor's list, and no jot or tittle of difference must there ever be. At least we knew where we were!

[2] The present writer remembers his keen disappointment when an attempt to form a school dramatic society was crushed at birth. This was in 1918.

live. Or, to put it otherwise, if we have ceased to learn, we have ceased effectively to live.

If we are to become a truly civilized people, we must accept and put into practice the principle that education should go on throughout life. The Report of 1919 on Adult Education looked forward to an enlightened and leisured society. Higher wages and shorter hours have not brought that day very much nearer. One of the obstacles to the better development of adult education in this country is the confusion as to what is, and what is not, 'adult education'. The 1919 Report unfortunately excluded 'technical or vocational' education. The distinction between liberal and vocational education is invalid, as A. N. Whitehead convincingly argued. The best education is, and has been, both. There is also in this country a customary but not very healthy distinction between recreational and educational activities at the adult level. The situation is happier in Canada and the USA, where adult education means quite simply the education of adults.[1]

Some years ago Dr Clark Kerr, President of the University of California, wrote that a university has three uses: undergraduate teaching, graduate teaching and research, and service activities for the general public. The third function is more generally recognized in America than in this country, though in recent years the universities (notably through drama and music) have been reaching out more effectively into the neighbourhood beyond their walls. Unfortunately our universities are still inclined to look upon their own extra-mural departments as fringe activities.

If education at the adult level is to meet the challenge of the future, we need more vision and more money. As Dr John Lowe wrote in a recent book: 'If the education of adults is to cease being a marginal national concern, it is now imperative that the government, the local authorities and the general public should begin to perceive it in its vast range and diversity, recognize its untapped potential as a source of community and national development, and accord it generous and sustained support.'[2]

---

[1] Something of the great variety of what adult education can mean is to be seen in the programmes and activities of a good Community Centre.

[2] John Lowe: *Adult Education in England and Wales: A Critical Review* (Michael Joseph, 1970). This is an up-to-date, authoritative survey of the work of the main agencies in the field of adult education: the DES, local authorities; evening institutes and adult centres; residential colleges, universities and the WEA; the public services (including the armed forces); women's organizations; other voluntary organizations; industry and commerce; broadcasting and films; libraries and art galleries.

BIBLIOGRAPHY

BREARLEY, M., et al., *A Teacher's Guide to Reading Piaget* (Routledge and Kegan Paul, 1966).
BÜHLER, C., *From Birth to Maturity* (Routledge and Kegan Paul, 1935).
CARMICHAEL, L. (ed.), *Manual of Child Psychology* (Chapman and Hall, 1954).
DEWEY, J., *Democracy and Education* (Macmillan, 1916; reprinted 1955).
FLAVELL, J. H., *The Developmental Psychology of Jean Piaget* (Van Nostrand, 1963).
HADFIELD, J. A., *Childhood and Adolescence* (Penguin, 1962).
ISAACS, S., *Intellectual Growth in Young Children* (Routledge and Kegan Paul, 1930; 8th Impression 1963).
ISAACS, S., *Social Development in Young Children* (Routledge and Kegan Paul, 1933; 9th Impression 1964).
KILPATRICK, W. H., *Education for a Changing Civilization* (Macmillan, 1926).
LOWE, J., *Adult Education in England and Wales: A Critical Review* (Michael Joseph, 1970).
MORRISH, I., *Education Since 1800* (Allen and Unwin, 1970).
PEEL, E. A., *The Psychological Basis of Education* (Oliver and Boyd, 1956).
PIAGET, J., *The Language and Thought of the Child* (Routledge and Kegan Paul, 1926; 3rd Revised Edition 1959).
REEVES, M. E., *Growing up in a Modern Society* (University of London Press, 4th Edition 1956).
SANDSTRÖM, C. I., *The Psychology of Childhood and Adolescence* (Penguin, 1966).
THORPE, L. P., *Child Psychology and Development* (Ronald Press, N.Y., 1955).
VALENTINE, C. W., *The Normal Child and some of his Abnormalities* (Penguin, 1956).

Chapter 5

Teaching and Learning

We have looked at education in terms of the tension between the individual and society, freedom and authority, continuity and change. There is tension also between teaching and learning.

It is not altogether cynical to see teaching and learning as opposed to one another. Children want to learn. They are full of curiosity, they want to explore the world and their own powers, they are enthusiastic adventurers. But the things they want to explore are often not the things which their teachers are trying to teach them. Hence the familiar contrast between the enthusiasm of the child's spontaneous approach to life and the boredom of his classroom resignation.

Not long ago the *Observer* sponsored a competition for secondary school children, in which essays on 'The School that I'd Like' were invited.[1] A boy of fifteen said roundly: 'My basic criticism of school is that pupils don't like it.' Some reached the level of poetry, as in the lament about the teaching that involves 'calling a leaf green instead of looking', and goes on:

> When I leave your school
> sitting at a dead desk
> I will forget
> What I mean ...

It is only fair to add that most of the entries revealed a willingness to learn.

Broadly speaking, boys and girls want to learn what will help them to achieve things that they want *now*, or in the easily foreseeable future: to be good at football, get a desired girl-friend, perhaps get a good job. The school curriculum does not, in their eyes, offer much that is relevant to these objectives. In the streets, in real life, you don't meet knowledge neatly packaged in 'subjects': history, geography and the rest. What have these 'subjects' to do with life as it is lived? On the other hand, if a boy needs some mathematics or physics in order to make or repair a model or piece of machinery in which he is interested, he will ransack the libraries until he gets it.

[1] Selections from the entries, edited by Edward Blishen, were published by Penguin, 1969, under the title *The School that I'd Like*.

The tension between learning and teaching is not merely the result of an academic curriculum. It is, in a sense, healthy to want to learn, but to dislike being taught. That is because, in the last resort, one cannot be taught; one can only teach oneself. One could almost define an educated person as one who has learnt to teach himself. The teacher can do no more than help one to learn; he cannot *make* one learn. It is impossible to teach someone who will not learn. There is a natural and right impulse towards creation and against being put into a mould. The pot has a right to argue with the potter. That does not mean that the teacher is superfluous, but only that the teacher's job is to help the pupil to learn, as the gardener's job is to help the plant to grow. That help is needed. It is impossible to learn without sources and means of learning, just as it is impossible to eat without food. The means of learning involve, at least in the early stages, the intervention of other people. Every animal begins parasitically, and man has a longer childhood than most animals.

Some tension – even conflict – between teacher and pupil is not only inevitable but has, within limits, a positive value. In Kenneth Barnes's words: 'Conflict between the adult and the child is not necessarily a bad thing. The really bad thing between the adult and the child is the absence of any emotional contact at all.'[1]

One of the most difficult things for a teacher (or a parent, for that matter) is to judge how to temper his control, or guidance, to the pupil's needs and capacity. As the pupil matures, he becomes able to do more for himself and needs less to be done for him. Gradually the teacher (or parent) must withdraw. There are no rules of thumb to tell the teacher when to withdraw, or let go. The teacher can let go too soon, or hang on too long; and in either case the result may be disaster. The conscientious teacher may be tempted to hang on too long, because he wants to be sure of producing the results that he has been working for – not only the satisfaction of good examination results, but (what is much more dangerous) the desire to see himself and his opinions mirrored in his pupils.

The teacher has a sacred duty to respect the legitimate autonomy of his pupils as persons. This does not mean that he must sit on the fence and never express strong opinions of his own. But it does mean that he must never use illegitimate means of influencing his pupils' thinking. And if the question is asked: What means of influencing other people's thinking are legitimate and what means are illegitimate? the short answer is that those means are legitimate which stimulate thought and those

---

[1] Kenneth Barnes in *Who Are the Progressives Now?*, by Maurice Ash, et al. (Routledge and Kegan Paul, 1969). Kenneth Barnes is headmaster of Wennington School, and author of *He and She*.

means which anaesthetize thought are illegitimate. It is a well-known device in political and commercial propaganda to present something in a way which *seems* to flatter the prospective customer's intelligence but which in reality puts him into an uncritically receptive state of mind. Herein is the difference between education and (in its pejorative sense) propaganda. It is a distinction which Sir Fred Clarke was fond of making a good many years ago; and it is vital to an understanding of what good teaching means.

The teacher must do his best to help his pupils in their own, sincere quest for truth, whether or not they end up in agreement with him. At the same time he must teach them that the right to an opinion has to be *earned*, by studying the subject. Freedom of thought does not mean the right to talk nonsense about something you know nothing about. The teacher is fully entitled to come down heavily on that kind of arrogance, notwithstanding Disraeli's remark that 'Every young man has a right to be conceited until he is successful'. The teacher's rightful authority is the authority of knowledge, experience and training, rather than the authority of status. And the wise teacher remembers that dignity, like a top-hat, is not improved by standing on it.

If the teacher is ever tempted to mount a pedestal, and to regard his pupils *de haut en bas*, he is likely to be brought to his senses by his pupils themselves. In any case he should remember that there is always a reciprocity between teacher and learner. If in a sense they pull against one another, in another sense they contribute to one another. Teaching is never all giving and learning all receiving. The teacher, if he succeeds in teaching anything, is bound to learn something from his pupils in the process. Nor can the pupil learn without giving something to the teacher. The teaching–learning relation is one in which both partners are being changed. And the more alive and effective the relation, the more will be given and received on both sides.

One of the most difficult tasks of a teacher is to combine personal interest with impartial justice. The more personally involved he becomes in the development of this or that child, the more difficult it becomes to avoid favouritism, and to give the time and trouble that each child needs. The least attractive, and least rewarding, pupil needs as much as those at the other end of the scale – perhaps more. There is a salutary warning in the schoolboy's comment on a new master: 'Well, at least he's *fair*. He hates the whole ruddy lot of us!' More seriously, the teacher has to learn, as Sir Fred Clarke used to put it, 'to care and not care'. It is not easy to be involved, and yet detached from one's own involvement; but it is part of a teacher's job.

Far more is known today about the learning process and the stages of growth than was known even half a century ago. But, like all science, the new knowledge has its limitations. If we are to make the best possible use of the new knowledge, we must know what those limitations are. We must keep our minds clear as to the sort of questions which the psychologist can answer and the sort of questions which he cannot answer. Broadly speaking, he can tell us how to achieve certain results, and what results are likely to follow from certain actions. What he cannot, *qua* psychologist, tell us is what educational aims are good and what evil. For example, if we want to educate people to think for themselves, the psychologist can help us. And if we want to condition people *not* to think for themselves, but to buy certain products or believe certain political doctrines, the psychologist can equally help us. In that sense, psychology is the genie of the lamp; and everything depends on who has the lamp.

More recent even than the era of the educational psychologist is the era of educational technology – the 'hardware' explosion of programmed learning, teaching-machines, video-tape and the rest. These devices can be of great educational value. There are things that teachers used to do (e.g. writing laboriously and dustily on blackboards) which can be better done by machinery. The hardware, properly used, can release teachers for higher and more human activities, and speed up the learning process. As in other departments of life, the machine can be of great value, provided man maintains his mastery of the machine. If man allows himself to be mastered by the machine, he is lost, in education or in anything else.

The same is true of the sciences as applied to education. Educational psychology is a good servant, but can be a bad master. Uncritical enthusiasm about means, and an unclear vision of ends, could easily result in a situation where our teaching and our research were dictated by the techniques at our disposal; where, in short, we would measure the things that we had the means of measuring. The next step is to assume that, because we can measure them, these are the things that matter.

The danger of allowing technology to become our master is picturesquely expressed by George B. Leonard: 'The Renaissance view of just who the devil was came clear in the legend of Faust: the devil, it turned out, was none other than the master technologist himself, the very same one who had led Adam and Eve out of their happy ignorance. To follow his forbidden knowledge as Faust did was to lose one's soul. This warning came at a time when new technology was shattering all the usual forms of existence throughout Europe. In the legend, the threatening technology was presented as old-fashioned medieval magic. Nothing surprising about this; as McLuhan has repeatedly pointed out, the content of each new environment is invariably the old environment itself; man drives into the future with his eyes fixed firmly on the rearview window.

'Christopher Marlowe in 1588 presented the Faust story in dramatic form, and his *Doctor Faustus* became immensely popular. Travelling troupes brought it even to small villages all across Europe. In several versions, including puppet plays, the traditional Faust story retained its popularity well into the nineteenth century, long after Goethe's literary treatment.'[1]

Mr Leonard goes on to refer to the story of *Frankenstein, or the Modern Prometheus*, written in 1818 by Mary Wollstonecraft at the age of nineteen, just after her marriage to the poet Shelley. A handbill advertising the dramatic version read: 'The striking moral exhibited in this story is the fatal consequence of that presumption which attempts to penetrate, beyond prescribed depths, into the mysteries of nature.'

There are, then, three possible responses to the opportunities of power offered by scientific discovery. Man may, like Faust, succumb to the lure of power, as power, and lose his soul, that is to say, lose his understanding of the real meaning of life. He may, in timid piety, renounce the dangerous knowledge and the possibilities it offers. Or, most difficult of all, he may welcome the new knowledge but try to remain its master.

Everyone who has thought deeply about education, from Plato to the present day, has known that learning is an activity – something that the learner does, not something that is done to him. In the last fifty years we have moved significantly towards practising what we have preached: not because we have been vouchsafed a clearer vision of the nature and purpose of education, but rather because some of the obstacles to effective education have been removed. These obstacles include lack of money, very large classes of children, inadequately trained teachers. In days when classes of ninety had to be kept in some sort of order, and the staffing of schools was eked out by pupil-teachers – only slightly removed in maturity from the monitors of Lancaster and Bell – schooling was inevitably pictured in terms of rows upon rows of (with luck) passive children, drilled in all their activities (including the right and wrong ways of holding pen or pencil), and moving in and out of the room by numbers. So long as classes remain as large as they are now, there is a case for 'streaming', on the grounds that the only hope of teaching a large number of children at once is to group them according to I.Q., so that they may be expected to progress at approximately the same rate. As the late Dr H. G. Stead pointed out thirty years ago, there is no educational virtue in 'streaming', which is simply an expedient to meet a practical situation.

Nowadays we picture schooling more in terms of free movement and dramatic expression. Perhaps we have swung too far in the direction of

[1] George B. Leonard: *Education and Ecstasy* (John Murray, 1968), published in England 1970.

informality. The old model-drawing was cramped and uninspired; but modern 'child art' is not everyone's cup of tea, especially when compared with recent studies of ape-art.[1] An activity may have diagnostic and/or cathartic value without being art. However that may be, freedom in education, properly understood, does not mean making things easy, but creating situations in which the children find the motive for making efforts.

We can never expect unanimity on the question of how free or how formal the teaching-situation should be. To a large extent, as will be suggested later, the issue is not so much an opposition of methods as a matter of the right stage at which discipline should be introduced into an activity. Nor should we ever forget that there is no point in talking about 'expression' unless there is something worth expressing. For the moment, the important fact is that school-children today are much more free to move about and express themselves than they were even a generation ago. This is especially true of primary education.[2]

Above the primary level class teaching is increasingly supplemented by group work and individual study. There is room for all three units of study. In the small group, one member can help another, individual jobs can be assigned and the results assembled. The individual, working alone, can often achieve far more than when harnessed in a team. The whole class provides a forum for surveying the total result. To take a simple example: a class of boys aged thirteen to fourteen may be studying the history of domestic architecture. Once a week in the school library they work individually and in groups of three or four on such topics as fortified castles, fortified and unfortified manor houses, eighteenth-century houses and parks. Once a term the whole class spends a week in workshops, and most of the boys will use this time in the construction of models. Once a year there is a conversazione, at which the class will put on an exhibition of models and charts, supplemented by short lectures, on domestic architecture. Incidentally, it is a notable fact that children will work much harder, and tackle more difficult problems, if their work is geared to a project with visible results. A group of boys writing a play about the trial and execution of Charles I, which was later performed in costume, dug into volumes of constitutional documents in order to find out exactly what charges were brought, and what was the defence. The class teacher, who kept in the background while these boys ransacked the library, would never have dared to put such difficult material before them in a routine classroom lesson.

[1] See *The Biology of Art*, by Desmond Morris (Methuen, 1966).
[2] See the Plowden Report: *Children and Their Primary Schools* (H.M.S.O., 1967). The forty-six photographs following p. 264 are a vivid documentation of modern ideas of primary education.

The increasing use of group work is a reminder that learning is very much a social activity. Much more is involved than a simple teacher-pupil relation. Learning depends also on relations between pupils, and on relations between pupils and their wider environment. The image of the school as an institution insulated from the world (as the schools of last century were physically separated by high walls and locked gates) is out of date. The school has moved out into the neighbourhood, and the neighbourhood is invited into the school.

It is often said that, if learning is to be effective, it must be geared to the child's present needs and interests, not to what we think he ought to have, or what we think may be useful to him some time hence, or what circumstances (e.g. in the form of examination requirements) impose upon us. There is truth in this view. But we must know what we mean when we talk of the child's present needs and interests. The doctrine certainly does not mean that the child should be left without guidance or inspiration. He may not know what his present needs are. Left to himself he may not be interested in anything, nor have any strong urge to do anything. He can be bored to tears by being left to his own devices. The story of the child in the 'progressive' school who asked: 'Have we got to do what we like again today?' is a salutary reminder that teaching is more than sitting back and waiting for something to happen.

What the doctrine of 'interest' really means is that the child, if he is to put his back into his work, must see his work as something worth doing – not as something that has to be done to avoid the consequences of not doing it. His work may be worth doing because it will equip him for a good job on leaving school, or quite simply because he enjoys that particular activity (whether it be gymnastics or painting, or even mathematics). Children are unpredictable creatures. The present writer once had a pupil whose ordinary class work was messy and muddled, but who had a passion for anything to do with ancient Egypt, and who made beautiful drawings which contrasted surprisingly with his handwriting. Again, a boy or girl may want to excel academically – perhaps to counterbalance a lack of distinction on the games field. There are, in fact, all kinds of motives that can make boys and girls work hard; and all kinds of motives for idleness. Few children are by nature lazy; the world is too interesting a place to ignore. The problem for the teacher is how best to awaken and arouse the child's interests, open up new worlds for him. Again, there are no rules of thumb. What can safely be said is that, the better the teacher knows his pupils as people, the more likely he is to be able to guide them into the paths of interest, knowledge, and – with luck – enchantment.

When we consider the content of learning (the curriculum), we have to notice a tension (already referred to) between direct, or raw, experience and formally organized knowledge.

On the one hand, it is obvious that life-experience does not come to us neatly packaged. In the street we do not encounter history, geography, chemistry, mathematics, *as such*; though we can scarcely do a piece of simple shopping without encountering them all. For the child, 'subjects' exist only in school, whereas in life things just happen. For the child this distinction between actual life and 'subjects' is perhaps the basic distinction between the world and school. It is not surprising that educators have been troubled by the gulf between learning and living, and have explored ways of making the school curriculum more real to the children.

On the other hand, if the human faculties are to function at all, experience has to be assimilated and organized. If we did no more with our experience than the other animals appear to do, we might develop habits and some emotional attitudes, but we should not *know* what we thought about our experience, or even *that* we thought about it; and certainly would not have anything that could be called a culture to pass on in such a way as to change society. In other words, we should have no history.

It is an essential part of each individual's education, as of every society's history, to assimilate his experience, analyse it, and organize it in coherent systems. There is nothing sacred or final about these systems of thought and knowledge, which we know in school and university as 'subjects'. They do in fact change through history, as human experience changes. In the Middle Ages, 'philosophy' included all that we know as the physical sciences – or rather, all that was then known of them. Sciences subdivide and new sciences arise, sometimes having to fight for a place on the map.[1]

But, although 'subjects' should be our intellectual servants, not masters, they are not arbitrary. One of the sources of confusion in the contemporary discussion of 'integrated curricula' is the misguided notion that 'subjects' are artificial. 'Subjects' arise from the fact that there are different orders of reality, different kinds of 'truth', and different kinds of 'proof' thereto appropriate. It has been well said that 'the subjects on the curriculum ... are there because among other things they initiate the pupil into the different modes of understanding that are characterized by distinct organizing concepts, principles of verification, and logical connections. Far from being merely conventional or arbitrary, they represent in their distinct disciplines of thought what it is to think, to know and to inquire.'[2]

---

[1] The present writer remembers, in the 1930s, a University Senate rejecting a proposal to establish a Department of Sociology, because there was insufficient agreement as to what constituted sociology.

[2] R. A. Pring: 'Curriculum Integration', *Bulletin*, Univ. of London Inst. of Educn., Spring, 1970.

A physicist, a painter, a theologian may look at a sunset. In terms of their own special interests, they will say very different things about the sunset, and use different languages in which to say it. To one of them, the sunset is a case of refraction of light; to another it is a gorgeous splash of colour; to the third it is an example of the overspill of divine bounty. The fact that the theologian is concerned with the proposition that God is good does not in any way invalidate the physicist's exposition of refraction. Nor do the physicist's operations prove anything whatever, one way or the other, about the existence or goodness of God.

When it comes to 'proof', we have to recognize that the procedure for establishing the 'truth' of propositions in different spheres of experience varies from one sphere to another. There is a proper procedure for examining and validating Pythagoras' Theorem, Boyle's Law, the Marxist interpretation of history, the opinion that Bach's music is good, the belief that God is Love; and in each case the procedure is different.

The traditional systems of thought and knowledge, then, are not arbitrary. And the systematic ordering of experience is a necessary human activity. There are, nevertheless, two problems of great educational importance.

One is the consequence of the enormous increase in human knowledge in modern times. We hear a good deal about 'excessive specialization'. This can be a misleading expression if it is taken to mean that there is something evil about intensive study. In one sense specialization cannot be excessive. What is meant by the expression is, rather, that, as specialists become increasingly absorbed in their own fields of study, these fields become smaller, and the specialists grow further apart from one another. Specialists are said to be people who know more and more about less and less. Specialists are accused of actually priding themselves on knowing nothing outside their own territory. And it has been said with some truth that, in our day, the problem is not that the biologist and the expert in Middle English speak different languages, but that two different kinds of biologist can no longer understand each other. If our civilization is to survive, we must somehow learn how to recover a coherent view of human thought and knowledge. At present our secondary and higher education does not stand up very well to that test.

The other educational problem is this. How can we best help boys and girls to understand the relation between raw experience and organized knowledge, so that they shall be equipped to transform the one into the other? Or, to put it differently, at what stage in the learning process is it right to impose order?

One of the contrasts between old-fashioned and modern teaching is that, as a general principle, we now hold back the formal discipline – the grammar of the subject – until the children have some familiarity with the material, and some interest in it. At one time, language-teaching began with declensions and conjugations, carpentry began with joints, music began with scales. In modern practice children are encouraged to communicate in the language, to make something of wood, to play some sort of tune. If the child responds at all to the situation, there will come a point when he will *need* discipline – technique – in order to perform well enough to satisfy himself. That is the point at which the grammar of the subject should come in. Creativity and discipline are not opposed to one another. Without discipline creation will never emerge from chaos. But the premature clamping down of discipline may crush creation at birth. Whether we are considering the acquisition of a particular skill, or the ordering of the map of human knowledge, the same problem arises: at what stage and by what means we should analyse and systematize.

These two problems, then (the one of managing the transition from experience to formulation, and the other of achieving a coherently inter-related view of the ever-expanding universe of knowledge), have stimulated modern thinking about curriculum and method. Logically, curriculum and method are distinct from each other, and it should be possible to discuss them separately. To some extent this is true in practice. But it is also true that they involve each other. To take a simple example: the 'project' or 'problem' method in any form involves a breakaway from tradition in both content and method.

There is nothing very new about attempts to plan both curriculum and methods of study in such a way as to give boys and girls a sense of the reality and relevance of what they study, and an insight into the contributions that different 'subjects' can make to a focal problem. It was in the early 1920s that Helen Parkhurst developed the Dalton Plan, by which the pupil undertook an assignment of work in various fields, to be completed in several weeks, and was free to budget his own time and consult teachers when necessary. It was William H. Kilpatrick (born 1871) who, shortly after the First World War, revived and re-presented Dewey's problem approach to learning under the name of the project method. By a 'project', Kilpatrick meant 'any unit of purposeful experience, any instance of purposeful activity, where the dominating purpose, as an inner urge, (i) fixes the aim of the action, (ii) guides its process, and (iii) furnishes its drive, its inner motivation'.

The pendulum has swung, not only away from the traditional formal curriculum, but back again to it, under the influence of political events. In the United States, the slump of the 1920s and, much later, the Russian Sputnik of 1957, both caused alarm lest secondary education was being allowed to become 'soft'.

In the past ten years or so in this country there has been a renewed concern about the secondary curriculum, and for several reasons. The extension and reorganization of secondary education forces us to ask what these pupils (including the 'Newsom children') are to learn. The early specialization forced upon the grammar schools by the competitive requirements for university entrance forces us to recognize that many of the more intelligent boys and girls are not getting anything like a balanced academic diet from perhaps the age of fifteen.[1] One way or another, it is generally acknowledged that our secondary curriculum has become somewhat chaotic – it has been described as a 'non-curriculum' – and needs to be thought out afresh.

A great deal of work, including practical experiment, has been done on curriculum in the last few years, not least under the auspices of the Schools Council.[2] The University of London Institute of Education has sponsored a number of studies in the field of Integrated Curriculum.[3] 'Integrated Curriculum' has, indeed, become a vogue term of late, and not all who use it are clear as to what they mean by it.

At a time when so many experimental reorganizations of curriculum are under discussion, this is not the place to attempt detailed examination of schemes proposed. What is more likely to be of use is to examine the assumptions underlying them. There is a danger that teachers may plunge into curricular adventures with the best of intentions but with no precise idea of what they are about. It has been said: 'There is a need for a much closer analytic and critical examination of "integrated" programmes if education is not to be sacrificed to yet more conceptual muddle and practical confusion.'[4]

The fact that some people talk of an 'integrated' curriculum, some of 'interdisciplinary' programmes, and others of 'open' and 'closed' aspects of the curriculum is in itself evidence of differing points of view. Those who prefer the term 'interdisciplinary' use it because they do not like the term 'integrated' – possibly because it may suggest an artificial smoothing-out

[1] It is notable that secondary education in France and Germany (the *baccalauréat* and the *abitur*) continues a broader subject-spread into the highest classes.

[2] Schools Council publications are listed in the Annual Report. Research projects at present on hand (March, 1970) include: Social Studies (8–13), The Whole Curriculum for the Middle Years of Schooling (8–13), Social Education Project (11–16), Project for the Integration of the Humanities (11–16), General Studies Project (15–18). In most cases these projects are sponsored by the Schools Council and the work is centred at a university.

[3] See particularly the Institute's *Bulletin* for autumn, 1969, and spring, 1970.

[4] R. A. Pring: 'Curriculum Integration', *Bulletin*, Univ. of London Inst. of Educn., spring, 1970.

of the varieties of knowledge. Those who prefer to talk of 'open' and 'closed' studies reject both the other terms, and seek to emphasize a flexibility of treatment by which, according to circumstances, broad interdisciplinary surveys can alternate with intensive concentration.

Some of the questions that ought to be asked at the outset of an experiment in curricular integration are the following:

(*a*) What are we seeking to integrate? The school curriculum? Society as a whole (a possible long-term result of sending out better-educated young people)? The individual pupil? The teaching staff? Or any combination of these? However we answer this question, it is as well to remember that, in the last resort, the only integrating factor is the human mind. And the only place where integration is any use is in the human mind. No educational programme is of the slightest use if it remains on paper.

(*b*) Assuming (as we safely can) that the aim of the whole operation is to promote as complete and coherent an understanding of human thought and knowledge as possible, are we to set about it by the more radical means of sweeping away the frontiers between 'subjects', or by the less radical method of accepting subjects, and groups of subjects, and trying to see the relations between them? If we take the more radical course, we must obviously beware of reducing knowledge to a formless pulp. If we take the less radical course, we must beware lest our 'integration' turns out to be nothing more than a series of perfunctory salutations over the garden walls. In any case we must recognize that our grand aim (of achieving a comprehensive survey of truth) is a vain hope, though we could certainly do a great deal better than we do now.

(*c*) Since no man can know everything, a workable curriculum must be selective. What principles should guide our selection of what goes in and what stays out? Shall we go for those branches of thought and knowledge which, at a high level, illuminate the meaning of human life (philosophy, religion, ethics, history, literature, pure science)? Or should we go for what is important at a much more pragmatic level: economics, technology, the mechanics of modern life? Or should we concern ourselves less with content and more with *modes* of thought and knowledge; should we seek to exemplify the different ways in which the human mind works: logical analysis (e.g. mathematics), empirical inference (e.g. physical science), moral and aesthetic value-judgements (ethics, the arts, religion)? This distinction between areas of knowledge and modes of thinking is a very important one, and may have great influence on the resulting curriculum. It may come to be the difference between snippets of this and that (some art and literature for the scientists and a smattering of science for the arts people) and an insight into the *nature* of the various subjects:

what is the physicist, the historian, etc., trying to do; and how does his work enrich humanity?

(*d*) How are we going to *present* the learning-situation? If we do not say: 'This is a Latin lesson', or 'This is geography', what do we say? Do we present a problem to be solved (e.g. how should industry and population be distributed?), or a project to be carried out (e.g. how can we help to relieve social need and distress in our neighbourhood?), or a broad topic to be explored (e.g. the rise and fall of civilizations)? And shall we pose practical problems (such as sex morality or labour unrest) or invite the examination, from various standpoints, of concepts such as democracy? In any case we must remember that, wherever we choose to lay the emphasis, practical projects and philosophical speculations are not ultimately separable from one another. Whether we are painting and papering an old-age pensioner's flat, or theorizing about the individual's responsibilities to the community, we are in the long run committed in both directions. Intelligent social behaviour should be backed by a social philosophy: that is to say, we should know why we are doing whatever we are doing. And a philosophy that never put forth fruit in action is a barren tree. Indeed, it is a characteristically academic error to picture thought as necessarily a preparation for action. More often than not it is action that promotes thought and brings understanding. 'If any man shall do his will, he shall know of the doctrine.'[1]

These are some of the questions that ought to be asked if we are to tackle intelligently the reorganization of the curriculum. It may be useful, as an illustration, to refer to one practical programme, recently proposed by Dr Denis Lawton, Senior Lecturer in Curricular Studies at the University of London Institute of Education.[2] Dr Lawton lays down two principles to guide the unified planning of curriculum: (*a*) The material should be 'a selection from the culture of a society to include those aspects of culture which are regarded as so important that they are entrusted to the school for expert transmission to the young'. (*b*) Having selected the material we want, we then have to 'organize these selections into learning situations'.

Discussing principles of selection, Dr Lawton rejects the single-core curriculum, on the grounds that it tends to be dominated by the core-subject: for example, science and social studies. He prefers an attempt to integrate a number of cores, derived from the forms of knowledge which have their different logics and ways of thought. He suggests the following five subject-groups, in each of which the pupil should reach a minimum level before going on to make choices.

[1] John vii. 17.
[2] Dr Denis Lawton, in *Bulletin*, Univ. of London Inst. of Educn., autumn, 1969.

(i) Mathematics.
(ii) The Sciences.[1]
(iii) The Humanities (including history, geography, classical studies, literature, religious studies).
(iv) The Expressive Arts (including P.E. as well as music, painting, drama).
(v) Moral Education.

The successful operation of such a curriculum, as Dr Lawton sees it, depends upon great flexibility of organization, of material, pupils, teachers, and time. There would be a departmental staff committee for each of the five areas, within which there would be close interrelation; there would be an over-all curriculum committee to look after the connections between the five areas; and there would be *ad hoc* groupings of teachers to work out particular interrelations of subject-groups. There would have to be flexibility of time-tabling, to enable projects to be carried through; and flexibility of pupil-grouping, to allow for team-work and individual study. There would also have to be more team-work among teachers, so that, for example, a team of teachers could work together on a topic with a year-group of pupils.

It is clear that the success or failure of programmes such as this must depend very greatly on the attitude of the teachers. They must cease to think of themselves as teachers of a particular subject, more or less insulated from others, and see themselves as contributing, from their own specialized angles, to a common enterprise. They must be alive, for example, to the relations between mathematics, physics and music, or (in a study of food supply or pollution) between ethics, politics, biology, and chemistry. One of the major difficulties about achieving this kind of ideal curriculum is that it makes very heavy demands on the teachers. One could almost go as far as to say that, provided the teachers are alive to their common aims and to the ways in which different subjects can support and supplement one another, the curriculum as set out on paper is of little importance. The present writer remembers a favourite saying of one of his senior colleagues forty years ago: 'The place for correlation' (it was called 'correlation' in those days, not integration) 'is in the staff room.'

So far this discussion of educational content has proceeded without use of the term 'liberal education'. This chapter can suitably end with

[1] Cf. the Nuffield Secondary Science Teaching Project (for pupils of 13–16) which is operating experimentally in 200 schools, based on Schools Council Working Paper No. 1. This scheme interrelates biology, physics, chemistry, and some technology.

some examination of what 'liberal education' means. The term is at least as old as Aristotle, and it is generally agreed that a liberal education is a good thing. What is not so generally agreed is what the term means.

Some confusion has arisen from the use of 'general education' as a synonym for liberal education. The famous Harvard Report of 1945 was entitled: *General Education in a Free Society*. In one sense a liberal education must be 'general', inasmuch as a liberally educated person should have a broad understanding of the world and human life. But it need not be general in the sense of encyclopaedic. The late Sir Richard Livingstone argued persuasively that Classical Studies (Greek and Roman language, literature and history) could provide a good liberal education.

Again, the issue has been confused by setting up 'liberal' in opposition to 'vocational' education. Professor A. N. Whitehead cogently argued that there is no necessary conflict between liberal and vocational education. Vocational education, taken broadly and humanely, can be as good personal education – and in that sense as liberal – as the classics. And the classics can be studied in such a way as to reduce them to a merely technical training for the teacher of more classics. A good education should be both liberal and vocational at the same time. It should help the student to understand man and the world, and also equip him to do some worthwhile job (otherwise it is merely dilettante). Indeed, if we think of the professional training of clergy, doctors and lawyers (the main preoccupation of the medieval universities), it is clear that education can be liberal and vocational at the same time. Equally vocational was the education of an eighteenth-century gentleman, whose classical studies were, in his day, a good political education for a member of the governing class. Nor is it only the learned professions of which this is true. A good craftsman, who understands his craft in its social and historical context, is also an educated man.

The apparent opposition between liberal and vocational education is to a large extent the result of social change. The Industrial Revolution created a new kind of workman – the machine-minder – and discouraged the older skilled craftsmanship. Meanwhile the spread of higher education to the intelligent sons of the working-class meant that these boys were receiving an education which was largely irrelevant to their needs, though it had been suitable enough for the gentry of an earlier age. Thus the gap widened between a 'liberal' education which was prestigious but useless, and a vocational education which was merely useful.

Historically the content of liberal education has expanded from the original core of the classics to include the rest of the humanities (literature, history, other languages, and so on). More recently the physical and social sciences have been brought in. It has been suggested that the contemporary expansion of the idea of liberal education to include the sciences is comparable with the humanist expansion at the time of the Renaissance.

Education is not 'liberal' because it includes a bit of everything; nor because it is of no practical use. What then is the distinctive principle of a liberal education?

In a recent essay,[1] Mr A. D. C. Peterson quotes these very modern words from Aristotle: 'People's views about education differ. There is no general agreement about what the young should learn ... Contemporary events have made the problem more difficult, and there is no certainty whether education should be primarily vocational, moral, or cultural. People have recommended all three ...' For Aristotle, liberal education meant the education proper for a free man: that is to say, an Athenian citizen, who had to be able to 'rule and be ruled by turns', patronize the arts, and in general play an active part in the many-sided life of the city state. The chores were done by slaves; and Aristotle expressly excluded from the free citizen's education everything 'banausic' – 'those arts which tend to deform the body ... and degrade the mind'. It is this rigid distinction between the slave and the free man which, historically, has led to the opposition between liberal and vocational education. This distinction is no longer relevant; and Mr Peterson accordingly amends Aristotle's description of a liberal education by echoing Francis Bacon's view that a liberal education is not so much one that is appropriate for a man who has the political status of a free citizen, but rather one that enables a man to free himself. That is to say, in terms of our own world and our own thinking, a liberal education is a *liberating* education.

When we go on to ask what should be the content of such an education, we must clearly look for an answer in terms of qualities and attitudes of mind, rather than of subject-matter. To quote Mr Peterson again, 'the aim of a liberal education is to develop the capacity for rational thought and true feeling rather than accumulate knowledge.'[2]

That is an important principle. But it does not dispose of the problem of curriculum-content. For we have to think and feel about *something*. And we find ourselves once more involved in the problem of selection of subject-matter. We must observe, however, that, in man's interaction with his experience through the centuries, certain conceptual frameworks have evolved. There is a natural reciprocity between experience and the human

[1] Concluding essay in *General Education: A Symposium on the Teaching of Non-Specialists*, edited by Michael Yudkin (Allen Lane, Penguin Press, 1969). A courageous group-effort, by writers who are nearly all university teachers, to pioneer a re-integration of thought and knowledge at university level because attempts to broaden sixth-form studies have so far had little result.

[2] Ibid.

mind. Our contemporary patterns of thought and knowledge are not final. But, as was suggested earlier in this chapter, they are good servants if bad masters; and we can use them to good effect provided we remember that the true end of education is quality of mind and not mere accumulation of knowledge.

To end this discussion with a chastening thought: educational practice is remarkably resistant to change. It is always hard for teachers to change their methods, their knowledge, their attitudes. They are mostly overworked, anyway; and it is as much as they can do to go on teaching what they know, in the ways they know. That is why so many well-meaning proposals for reform of the curriculum have come to nought. Mr Peterson reminds us that, in the ten years since the publication of the Crowther Report of 1959, there have been six proposals for reform, two individual and four resulting from committees. Five of these were rejected, four by the schools and one by the universities. Prophetically he adds: 'It is almost inevitable that by the time these words are printed the schools will have rejected the sixth' (the Dainton recommendations).

BIBLIOGRAPHY

ASH, M., *et al.*, *Who Are the Progressives Now?* (Routledge and Kegan Paul, 1969).
AYERST, D., *Understanding Schools* (Penguin, 1967).
BLISHEN, E., *The School That I'd Like* (Penguin, 1969).
BORGER, R., *et al.*, *The Psychology of Learning* (Penguin, 1966).
BROWN, J. A. C., *Techniques of Persuasion* (Penguin, 1963).
D.E.S., *Children and Their Primary Schools* (Plowden Report) (H.M.S.O., 1967).
FLEMING, C. M., *Teaching: A Psychological Analysis* (Methuen, 1958).
HILGARD, E. R., *Theories of Learning* (Appleton-Century-Crofts, 1948).
KILPATRICK, W. H., *Foundations of Method* (Macmillan, 1925).
OLSON, W. C., *Psychological Foundations of the Curriculum* (Publication No. 26) (Unesco, Paris, 1957).
PETERSON, A. D. C., *The Future of Education* (Cresset Press, 1968).
PINSENT, A., *The Principles of Teaching-Method* (Harrap, 3rd Edition 1969).
THOMSON, R., *The Psychology of Thinking* (Penguin, 1959).
WHEELER, D. K., *Curriculum Process* (Univ. of London Press, 1967).
YUDKIN, M. (ed.), *General Education: A Symposium on the Teaching of Non-Specialists* (Allen Lane, Penguin Press, 1969).

Schools Council Publications (H.M.S.O.)
A. WORKING PAPERS:
No. 10 *Curriculum Development: Teachers' Groups and Centres*, 1967.

No. 11 *Society and the Young School Leaver: Humanities Programme*, 1967.
No. 12 *The Educational Implications of Social and Economic Change*, 1967.
No. 17 *Community Service and the Curriculum*, 1968.
No. 21 *The 1966 C.S.E. Monitoring Experiment*, 1969.
No. 22 *The Middle Years of Schooling from 8 to 13*, 1969.

B. OTHER SCHOOLS COUNCIL PUBLICATIONS:
The New Curriculum, 1967.
Humanities for the Young School Leaver: An Approach through English, 1968.

Chapter 6

Fact and Feeling: Kinds of Truth

The purpose of this chapter is to examine two important distinctions and their educational implications. One is the distinction between two kinds of knowing or awareness, which we may call intuitive and articulated, or, if we prefer, existential and conceptual. The other is a distinction, *within* articulated or conceptual knowledge, between statements of fact and judgements of value. We shall see, as we did when considering other pairs of terms, that these distinctions involve elements of tension.

We can begin with some simple examples of awareness. I see a pillar-box, or my neighbour putting something into his dustbin, or I hear a dog barking. It would generally be agreed that such an act of awareness is a relation between the observing subject and an observed object. *I* am aware of *something*. And that something is 'given'; I do not constitute it. This is true, even when I voluntarily call up a memory or an image. There is no creation *ex nihilo*; the object recalled is either something previously experienced or something constructed (like the strange beasts of mythology) of elements taken from things previously experienced. It is equally true when the object of awareness is a feeling of my own – such as a headache. If I say: 'I have a headache', the 'I' is not the pain, although it is *my* pain. I say: 'I *have* a headache', not: 'I *am* a headache'.[1]

Any act of awareness, then, implies a relation between an observing subject and an observed object. The next thing to notice is that the act is a complex one. Indeed, the examples given in the previous paragraph, which were described as 'simple', are only comparatively so. The statement: 'I see a pillar-box' involves, not only sensory perceptions of shape and colour, but a good deal of previous experience, from which I have learnt to abstract a recognizable concept, pillar-box, from encounters with pillar-boxes of various shapes, colours and sizes. What in fact we observe, in an act of awareness, is a *gestalt* – a complex of interrelated parts. And we can voluntarily vary the spread of attention, so as to take in (as a meaningful whole) more or less of what is before us. I can,

---

[1] There may be disturbed mental states in which the distinction between the observing self and the observed object is blurred – when, for the moment at least, I *am* the headache. But such exceptions only serve to prove the rule.

for example, observe my-neighbour-putting-something-into-his-dustbin, a familiar sight to which I give only fringe attention and dismiss. Or I may observe that the dustbin is a new one, thereby extracting the dustbin from the *gestalt* and making it a thing-in-itself. I can go further, and break down the dustbin into elements: lid, handles, and so on. The power of seeing things together, and of selecting what we see together and what we separate, is basic to awareness as we know it.

Our normal observations, even of everyday objects, are so complex that we may well ask whether there is such a thing as a truly 'simple' act of awareness. Whether it is possible to answer this question or not, the inquiry is useful because it opens up the first important distinction with which this chapter is concerned.

Suppose I have a sudden, unexpected stab of pain in my hand while I am weeding a flower-bed, with my thoughts on quite other matters. I instantly withdraw my hand, with an involuntary exclamation. In retrospect I can see that there was a moment when the stab of pain was all that I was aware of. It was only later that, after examining my hand and recalling relevant knowledge, I was able to tell myself that I had been stung by a bee, probably one of the solitary species that burrows in the earth.

The following example is interesting because it illustrates our likeness to the other animals as well as our difference from them. I was walking in the New Forest, along a familiar path, paying little attention to my immediate surroundings, but thinking about some writing that I was engaged upon. Suddenly something happened, which I can only liken to an emotional explosion, which threw me several paces backwards, away from an equally sudden movement in the opposite direction. For an instant that was all I knew. Then I was aware of the thumping of my heart and a sense of alarm. Next came the realization that I had almost walked into a pony which was half asleep and scarcely visible in the shadow of a hawthorn tree. The pony had sprung away from me in fear. I had jumped back from the pony's sudden movement. As soon as I knew what had happened, I went forward again, and made reassuring noises to the pony. But the pony would not be comforted, and trotted away from me. That was the difference between the human and the animal response. Our first, immediate reactions were equal and opposite. But the pony continued its intuitive avoiding action. The complete change in my own behaviour was due to the fact that I had *understood,* that is to say, I had been able to tell myself what had happened, and plan my next move in the light of that knowledge.

In a human act of awareness there are two elements. One, which we share with the other animals, is an immediate, intuitive apprehension, which is sufficient to spark off accurate and discriminating action, but does not involve making statements to oneself about what has happened, i.e. analysis and synthesis.

The other element – the conceptual one – consists in telling oneself what has happened, using the power of abstraction to analyse and synthesize, and make propositions using symbols. Without the power of abstraction and the use of symbols (the most familiar of which are words) we could not *think* – or, at least, we could not know whether or what we thought. But without the primary, intuitive experience, there would be nothing to think *about* and no impulse to think.

If we consider the relation between these two kinds of awareness, it is obvious that we depend on conceptual thinking for all the 'higher' intellectual activities of man. Without it there could be no science, no history, no philosophy. The whole structure of thought and knowledge rests upon the power to make abstractions, to analyse and synthesize, and to formulate. There could not otherwise be a system of advanced nuclear physics, or a police record of a wanted man, or, for that matter, a weekly shopping list. It should be noted that, although reference was made to the 'higher' intellectual activities, conceptual thinking (by means of abstractions) is not *superior* to existential knowing. The person-to-person knowledge of a friend is something deeper and of greater value than any information *about* him that could be recorded.

To be fully human we need both kinds of knowing. And, although there could be no systems of thought and knowledge without conceptual thinking, we must beware of losing contact with existential experience. Conceptual thinking can be a handicap, or barrier, luring us away from face-to-face confrontation with raw experience into a tidy, antiseptic world of ideas, where the theologian can go through the motions untouched by conscience, or the sociologist happily operates a shadow-show of human statistics.

Although the temptation to escape from reality into abstraction is one to which academic people are specially exposed, it is also a common human danger. Near the beginning of Chapter 5 the child's lament was quoted about the kind of teaching that involves 'calling a leaf green instead of looking'. There is a sense in which abstraction is the lazy man's way of thinking – or even of not thinking. The expression 'population explosion' saves us from the tremendous effort of trying to get our imaginations round the human realities of 3,000 million people going on breeding and needing food. A phrase like 'the under-privileged' comfortably shortcircuits a good deal of emotional effort. In medical work it is easier to deal with 'cases' than with people. It is surely no accident that the present age of unprecedented power of public communication is also an age of cliché-tyranny.[1] When the imagination boggles, it takes refuge in labels.

The myth of the Fall of Man could be taken as an allegory of the passage from the primeval innocence of immediate intuitive experience into the sophisticated, but endlessly frustrating, world of conceptual thought. And, in this context, the Christian teaching that the Kingdom is for those who come as children, and that we must be born again, could be taken to mean that we must continually return to, and rediscover, the intuitive awareness which underlies and tends to be submerged by our conceptual thinking.

Symbols, whether verbal or other, have an ambivalent function. They can (as we have seen) remove us from immediate awareness of the things they represent. In that way they not only provide a shorthand which makes possible all the sciences and other systems of knowledge; they can also save us the trouble of coming to grips with direct experience. But – and this is the interesting thing – they can also re-create, re-vivify, the primary experience. To perform this kind of revelation seems to be one important function of art.

Aesthetic theory is a very difficult and controversial territory, and one into which it is foolish to rush. But, without attempting anything like an answer to the question: What is Art?, we may reasonably suggest that art has this very important role – in a sense a redemptive role – of bridging the gap between original, intuitive awareness and conceptual thought. One could say, rather, that in art there is no such gap – that in art the distinction between intuitive awareness and conceptual thought is transcended, so that the primal awareness is embodied, a unique moment preserved for ever.[2]

Let us look further at these two aspects of art. On the one side, by means of skilful use of imagery – musical, pictorial, verbal – art recaptures the quality of immediate intuitive perception, with the intensity and excitement which an experience may have had once and for all long ago. To take a simple example, a child of seven is taken to church for the first time one Easter morning in the country. The dew is still on the primroses in the mossy banks. The sound of the church bells tumbles through the warm spring sunshine. There is in fact nothing unique, nothing even remarkable, about that morning. Church bells, spring sunshine, primroses,

---

[1] See Mario Pei: *Words in Sheep's Clothing* (Allen and Unwin, 1970). Among other diseases of language, Professor Pei discusses the debilitating effect of euphemism. A 'credibility gap' means a lie. 'Peace' means the cessation of all opposition to your own side of the conflict; and 'aggression' means any resistance to you and what you stand for.

[2] Cf. Rossetti's phrase, 'A Sonnet is a moment's monument.'

are commonplace enough. Nevertheless, that particular experience *was* unique, for that small boy. It had a quality of enchantment which, in the sixty years that have passed since then, he has never been able to express adequately, nor to recapture, and he has never had that experience again. It is one of the things that he will go on groping after to the end of time. What art can do is to recapture such experiences, and give them life, not as it were photographically, but by all kinds of evocative imagery. In a simple example, a poet might, with magic of words, re-create the lost enchantment of the small boy's Easter morning. As a more complex example, religious symbolism, by picture, music, ritual, language, may express and communicate the rich variety of feeling: love, joy, peace, longsuffering, and the other gifts of the Spirit.

Not only does art re-create the primary intuitive experience; it also gives it lasting embodiment, places it on record so to speak, so that it is permanently available. Moreover, the work of art objectifies the experience, in the sense that it places us in the position of spectators – privileged perhaps, but not actively engaged in the original experience – 'emotion recollected in tranquillity'. Because of this objectivity we can reflect upon the experience; we can intuit and philosophize at the same time. We are indeed invited to do so. And we may be *more* intensely aware of the experience than we could be if actually having it, because direct involvement would include feelings that were irrelevant to the quality of the experience itself. An example might be a good battle film, in which we can be more poignantly aware of the horrors of war than if we were taking part (for we would then be too frightened, or just too numb, to know what we were feeling).

It has nevertheless to be recognized that artistic (e.g. dramatic) presentation can diminish as well as intensify feeling. We may idly half-watch a Western, bullets and arrows flying, and placidly munch a sandwich, knowing that it is only a film anyway. In fact, this kind of entertainment is not *intended* to harrow our feelings. What effect a work of art will have – whether to intensify or dilute feeling – depends on various things, including the purpose and quality of the work of art. It may be intended only as a light breeze titillating the surface of our emotions; or it may fail to stir us deeply because it is badly done. The effect also depends on the mood and circumstances of the observer. We respond more readily to some things than to others. People who keep dogs will have noticed that their pets, having remained unmoved throughout some thrilling drama on the telly, will be instantly activated if a dog barks on the screen.

Keats' *Sonnet to Sleep* is a good example of the power of art to re-create the awareness of primary or existential experience. The means used are complex. The rhythm of the verse rocks the cradled reader's mind. There is a wealth of imagery and association – 'soft embalmer of the still midnight', 'our gloom-pleased eyes, embowered from the light' – a whole pageant of Morpheus. And there is the sound of the words themselves, sinking to silence in the last two lines:

> Turn the key deftly in the oiléd wards,
> And seal the hushéd casket of my soul.

To read and ponder that poem is to deepen and establish all that we already know about sleep.

The evocative power of art is most easily discussed in terms of language. But the same kind of thing happens in painting, music and dance. Music and painting can range from representational description at one end of the scale to pure pattern-making at the other. But even at both these extremes art has the double character of re-creating experience and inviting reflection upon it. The most 'photographic' painting has something that the camera could not have produced; and the most imitative music is distinguishable from what it imitates. At the other end of the scale the pure pattern of shapes and colours, or of sounds, has some reference to life-experience inasmuch as it evokes a state of feeling, a mood; it has meaning, as distinct from something accidental.[1] In short, all art evokes experience and makes or invites comment on that experience. In that way art brings into relation with each other the two kinds of awareness that were distinguished earlier.

Before going on to the second main distinction with which this chapter is concerned, we ought to look at some of the educational implications of what has been already said.

In Chapter 5 there was some discussion of the contrast between the immediacy of life-experience and the remoteness of academic 'subjects': a contrast which is pointed by the child's protest against 'calling a leaf green instead of looking'. It is an important part of education to give children plenty of opportunity for direct experience, sensory and emotional, as well as for reflecting on experience and organizing their ideas.

In the last hundred years we have moved a long way towards recognizing the educational value of direct experience – of sense, feeling, action as means of apprehending and coming to terms with our world. In the schools of the mid-nineteenth century, the tyranny of abstraction was extreme. The Newcastle Report records this comment from an inspector: 'I find nothing commoner than a knowledge of such facts as the weight of Goliath's spear, the length of Noah's ark, the dimensions of Solomon's

---

[1] If it evokes nothing, we are entitled to say that it is not art – at least as far as we are concerned.

temple, what God said to David or what Samuel did to Agag by children who can neither explain the commandments, the sacraments or the parables with moderate intelligence, or tell you the practical teaching of Christ's life.' Another inspector reported that a certain school prided itself on its history teaching, the chief attainment of the boys being to repeat the names and dates of the kings of England very fast and correctly *backwards* from Queen Victoria.

One of the few available books, *A Short System of Polite Learning*, had questions and answers of the following type:

Q. What is Astronomy?
A. A mixed mathematical science; teaching the knowledge of the celestial bodies, their magnitudes, motions, distances, periods, eclipses and order.

It was constantly noted that children learnt to read aloud without the slightest understanding of what they read. For example, an inspector tells of a boy who read from Matthew ix how Jesus entered into a ship, and passed over, and came into his own city; but the boy was unable to say what Jesus entered into or came into.[1]

We have moved a long way from this kind of instruction. And, in contrast, it is no bad thing to look again at the lively photographs in the Plowden Report. But we have no reason for complacency. Without succumbing to the extreme excesses of the heuristic method (which would have excluded all knowledge which the children did not discover by original investigation) we nevertheless have to recognize that our teaching (especially at post-primary level) is still weighted on the side of conceptual operations as contrasted with sensory and emotional experience – partly because of the pressure of syllabuses and examinations, and partly because it is easier to get children to memorize formulae than to help them into the experience from which the formulae are derived.

Our secondary and higher education is still too intellectualistic in emphasis. To say this is not to denigrate the intellect. When Lord Morley said: 'An educated man is one who knows when a thing is proved and when it is not', he was expressing a very important truth about education. But it is not the whole truth. The full aim of education is better conveyed in the Greek καλοκἀγαθία, nobleness – a union of beauty and goodness. In a balanced system of education, two things need to be watched. First, in those studies which properly issue in conceptual systems of knowledge (*par excellence* the sciences) there should be enough direct contact with the material, by observation and experiment, to support the theoretical

---

[1] These examples are taken from among many more in Dr M. Sturt's *The Education of the People* (Routledge and Kegan Paul, 1967).

structure, so that the children can 'get the feel' of the subject.[1] Secondly, studies which properly issue in conceptual systems should not outweigh those activities in which sense, feeling and movement are central, that is to say, physical exercise, the arts, including drama and symbolic ritual. We must, in fact, as we have so long protested, try to educate the whole child.

The most important kind of immediate, existential experience is in personal relations. Personal relations transcend, rather than defy, abstract formulation. There is indeed a great deal about a person that can be formulated, measured, docketed. But the sum of these data is always something less than the person. John Smith's police dossier may be accurate, as far as it goes, but it is not John Smith. And, if John Smith is a friend of mine, I *know* him in a way to which the data in the dossier are irrelevant. I may even be unable to supply some of the information that the police have collected about John Smith. I am not interested in his height or weight; I may be uncertain about the colour of his eyes. But I *know* John Smith.[2]

One of the most important things that education can do is to encourage person-to-person contacts, so that persons can enrich their direct experience of other persons. The teacher–pupil relation, in particular, should as far as possible be a personal, not merely a formal, one. This means that the teacher must be prepared to give of himself, yet without being over-possessive. That is why teaching is a very demanding, and fairly exhausting, profession. Something was said about personal relations in Chapter 2. It is essentially in and through relations between persons that persons grow.

There is an interesting legend which illustrates the value of personal relations. Christ, at his Ascension, was met by the Archangel at the Gates of Heaven. The Archangel asked him what plans he had made for the furtherance of his Kingdom on earth. Christ answered: 'I have left eleven men.' 'And,' said Gabriel, 'what if they fail?' 'I have made no other plans,' said Christ.

The second of the two main distinctions with which this chapter is concerned is within the field of conceptual knowledge. It is the distinction between a statement of fact and a judgement of value, each of which has

---

[1] For example, it is not much use teaching the Industrial Revolution in terms of textile manufactures to children who have never seen a cotton-mill.

[2] The portrait-painter, or caricaturist, must try to catch the existential personal quality (the 'character') of his subject, and must also formulate it so as to be able to convey it in line and colour. Here again, art bridges the two kinds of awareness.

its own kind of truth (or untruth). 'It is raining' is a factual statement. So also is: 'It will probably rain tomorrow.' On the other hand: 'People ought not to do that sort of thing' is a value-judgement.

Before going further we should notice that the *form* of a proposition may be misleading. The statement 'God is Love' is factual in form; but it is not really a factual statement. Rather it is a judgement about the nature and purpose of existence. 'There goes the guilty man!' may be either a factual statement, if his guilt has been established, or is likely to be established, in a court of law, or a value-judgement, if it means, 'I disapprove of what he has done.'

Statements of fact (which William McDougall would have classed as 'cognitive' operations) are ways of saying that something is the case – and it is the case irrespective of the observer's attitude of mind. The fact that the rain is falling has nothing to do with my pleasure or displeasure, approval or disapproval, whether I want to mow the lawn or welcome a shower on my lettuces. Factual statements are the building-material of the sciences. They are also at the heart of the administration of justice. The 'truth' of all such statements has to be established, in the legal phrase, 'beyond all reasonable doubt'. What degree of doubt we can tolerate, or what measure of certainty we require, depends on the circumstances and the nature of the evidence that can be brought. In the chemistry laboratory, because our evidence is precisely controlled under experimental conditions, we can get, and require, a very high degree of certainty. There is always the remote possibility that we may have made mistakes in our measurements, or that, if we did the experiment once more, we might get a different result. And such scientific revolutions as the change from Newtonian to Einsteinian physics, and the changes in cosmology, remind us that physical science is not infallible. Nevertheless, we can take the physical sciences as illustrating the kind of factual statements in which 'reasonable doubt' is minimal.

When we turn to the administration of justice, we are dealing with situations where we cannot expect the degree of certainty which is required in the science laboratory. Notwithstanding the development of forensic science, we are largely dependent on the human element. 'Beyond all reasonable doubt' becomes a more elastic term, and we often have to be satisfied with strong probabilities. This is not because the issues at stake are less important. The fate of the prisoner in the dock is probably vastly more important than the concoction bubbling in a test-tube in the laboratory. But, in the nature of the case, we cannot always have cast-iron proof in the law courts. Witnesses are notoriously unreliable, and perhaps not always honest. Sometimes we have to rely on circumstantial evidence.

If we move from the law courts to the work of the sociologist or historian, for example, we see that 'reasonable doubt' becomes still more elastic. Not that there can be any serious doubt of recent population statistics, or of the existence of Oliver Cromwell. But workers in these fields have to *interpret* their data, in terms of reasonable expectations, probable causes and results, and so on. Here, although respectable scholarship demands substantial evidence, there is room for disagreement among experts. And if the sociologist or historian never allowed himself to say anything that would not stand up in a court of law or a chemistry laboratory, he might have very little to say; at all events, his contribution to human thought would be much impoverished.

From the most inexorable scientific discipline to the sensational rumour of the press reporter, all factual statements have this character in common: that they offer information, or what purports to be information, about something. They say that this is, or is not, so.

It is sometimes supposed, because science rests on empirical evidence, and scientific statements are empirical in form, that science is entirely empirical in its processes. The truth is that science – and so do all factual propositions for that matter – involves a great deal that is not empirical. These non-empirical elements are presuppositions, assumptions, of various kinds, including the laws of logic.

The results of scientific investigation are normally set out inductively – that is, as if science proceeded inexorably from empirical data to inferred conclusion. Experiments are carried out, observations are made, and scientific laws are formulated on the basis of the data. In point of fact, scientific discovery seldom happens like that. Most important scientific advances involve a leap in the dark: a guess, an inspiration, a revelation if one may use the word. The detective investigating a crime often starts with a hunch, though he must finish up with systematically arranged evidence. The scientist usually calls his hunches hypotheses; but they are acts of faith nonetheless. Newton's guess that the principle behind the falling apple was the principle behind the whole sidereal universe was an inspired hunch which required a great deal of subsequent experimental and observational data to confirm it. Revelation and acts of faith are not the monopoly of religious experience; scientists depend on them whether they like it or not.

Not only does scientific discovery involve leaps in the dark, but all scientific systems presuppose certain *categories*, without which they cannot operate. Not only does the scientist assume the validity of sense-perception and of logical argument; he also has to assume certain principles of interpretation, such as cause and effect. We can observe *post hoc*. But the belief that, in any situation, *post hoc* is *propter hoc* is one which, however reasonable and necessary for sane thinking, can never be proved by the methods of science.

Another category which is normally assumed is that of time. Time is a more mysterious thing than is usually supposed. We habitually think of time as a succession of static instants, following one another like the ticks of a clock. Henri Bergson pointed out that this notion of time (assumed in scientific work and in everyday practice) excludes the possibility of choice, which we also take for granted in ordinary life. Our concrete, or existential, experience is not of a succession of separate events, but of continuous change. Freedom, and therefore choice, are directly known in the continuous flow of activity. Choice implies an appreciation of the *meaning* of a situation as a whole, in which past, present and future are embraced, and something can be done which makes the future different from what it might otherwise have been. If we envisage a series of separate events, each depending on the one before, like the impact of shunting travelling the length of a goods train, we are imprisoning ourselves within a determinist system which excludes choice. In other words, doctrines of freedom and determinism tell us at least as much about the way in which we look at reality as they do about the nature of reality itself.

Again, any field of inquiry is defined by limiting terms of reference. If, like the Behaviourists, we look at human behaviour in terms of stimulus-and-response, that is what we shall find. If we limit our inquiry to the chemistry of human behaviour, we must not be surprised if we discover nothing in man but chemistry. We have, in that case, no right to say that man is nothing but complicated chemistry, or that he has no soul, because we couldn't find one. For we have, by the structure of our inquiry, made it impossible to find anything outside our terms of reference. In all investigation, you get out what you put in; and you cannot get out what you don't put in. By all means let us assume, with the Freudians, that God is a projection of the super-ego. We shall doubtless find super-egos projecting themselves like mad. But that is all we shall find. We must never expect an interpretation to declare its own inadequacy. If we suspect that there may be more in heaven and earth than our researches have revealed, we must enlarge our terms of reference. Which is only a pedestrian way of stating Augustine's paradox: 'Crede ut intellegas' – 'Believe in order that you may understand'. Take an imaginative chance, as Newton did; and it may pay off. Search the heavens, metaphorically as well as astronomically, and you may penetrate the depths of Reality. Stick like a caterpillar to its leaf, and you will never know more than a leaf – at least, not until you hatch from your chrysalis.

It is, of course, necessary for systematic discovery, and for sane living, that we should limit our terms of reference according to circumstance. In a court of law, a question of law has to be determined; and this is often a different thing from a question of ethics. The only result of blurring the distinction between the law and the dictates of conscience would be bad administration of the law.[1] What has been said in the previous paragraph is not meant to belittle the importance of carefully defining the terms of reference of any field of study. Such definition is necessary to intellectual discipline. Our concern is rather with the importance of remembering what our terms of reference are, and the dangers of muddled thinking that result from forgetting the limitations that we have imposed. As was suggested in an earlier chapter, clear thinking depends largely on knowing what kinds of questions the various branches of human thought and knowledge are entitled to ask, and in what terms they are equipped to give answers.

The word 'feeling', which was used in the title of this chapter, is a very ambiguous term. Feeling heat or cold is different from feeling that this or that is right or wrong, or beautiful. We can further distinguish the feeling that we *like* a beautiful thing from our feeling that it is beautiful. More obviously, we can distinguish between our feeling that a certain course of action is right from our desire, or lack of it, to pursue that course of action.

That which is to be contrasted with a statement of fact is a judgement of value, which may be described as a 'feeling' inasmuch as it is not only a statement but, in a sense, an *act*, in which we commit ourselves in a way that brings us under judgement. If I say: 'It is raining', I tell you nothing about myself – what kind of person I am. But if I say: 'That was a rotten thing to do', I reveal my own nature. Fact certainly enters into value; we need information before we can judge an action to be good or evil. But the value-judgement is different from any knowledge of fact. To use William McDougall's terms again, a value-judgement takes us beyond the purely cognitive into the region of affective and conative experience.

Before going further, we should note that the modern prestige of science has put value-judgements at a disadvantage. Ethical beliefs and attitudes seem uncertain, unprovable, possibly meaningless, as compared with scientific discoveries. In this connection it is significant that, at one time, the Logical Positivist philosophers were saying that value-statements were meaningless, because not empirically verifiable. During the last twenty years or so, however, they have somewhat changed their tune. They now allow that value-statements have meaning, but say that they are prescriptive, not descriptive, statements. Professor A. J. Ayer exemplifies this point of view. But to say that a value-judgement is prescriptive rather

[1] This is something of which juries have to be reminded.

than descriptive does nothing to remove, or to answer, the really important question of whether the judgement is *valid*. It is the source and validity of values that matters.

Although ethical value is only one kind of value, it will be convenient for the present purpose to limit the discussion to this category.

The first thing to notice is the ambiguity of the word 'good'. Aspirin is good for headaches. Our M.P. is a good speaker. Our vicar is a good man. Walking is good exercise. A good child is one that doesn't give trouble. Broadly, we can distinguish between instrumental values and intrinsic values. Aspirin and walking are instrumentally good: that is, they are means to some predetermined end – the cure of a headache, the maintenance of physical fitness. Physical fitness itself may be seen instrumentally, as we are reminded in the old story of the man who said: 'I must keep fit', and got the answer: 'Fit for what?' On the other hand, walking may in some circumstances have intrinsic values. Some people walk for sheer enjoyment. It all depends on whether one walks because one likes walking, or because one thinks one needs exercise or has no other means of getting from *A* to *B*.

It is when we enter the realm of intrinsic values, things that are good in and for themselves, that we are concerned with ethics. Not all intrinsic values are ethical (there is nothing ethical about walking because one enjoys walking, or driving a car because one enjoys driving). But all ethical values are either intrinsic or are demonstrably connected with values that are good in themselves. Throughout history men have believed that there are qualities, such as unselfishness, courage, loyalty, which have value-in-themselves. Philosophers have not agreed, however, as to what is the ultimate intrinsic value, the supreme good. The Greeks spoke of virtue. St Paul wrote of the gifts of the Spirit: love, joy, peace, and the rest. The idealist speaks of self-fulfilment, or, simply, goodness. But the hedonist's ultimate value is pleasure.

Before going further, it will be as well to dispose of the fallacy of hedonism, as held by the Utilitarians. Psychological hedonism holds that what a man desires is his pleasure. The fallacy is that we do not desire the *pleasure*, but the *thing* that gives us pleasure. A glass of beer may give me pleasure; but what I want is beer, not pleasure. Ethical hedonism holds that a man can desire, and ought only to desire, his pleasure. But to say that is to beg the question of the meaning of 'ought'. If there is nothing in the equation but pleasure, the importation of 'ought' is unnecessary and confusing. If, on the other hand, the term 'ought' is needed, we have abandoned pure hedonism.

A further complication of the Utilitarian position (as formulated by Jeremy Bentham) is the proposition that the ultimate criterion is the greatest happiness of the greatest number. It is illogical to jump from *my* pleasure to other people's pleasure. If my only concern is my own pleasure, the pleasure of others is irrelevant except in so far as it may contribute to mine; the pleasure of others has no intrinsic value for *me*.

Yet another difficulty of the hedonist position is that there is no recognizable measure of pleasure. As Bentham put it: 'Quantity of pleasures being equal, pushpenny is as good as poetry.' Since common sense revolts against this proposition, it is natural to allow that there are *qualities* as well as quantities of pleasure. John Stuart Mill did indeed admit kinds as well as degrees of pleasure. But, by doing so, he capsized the whole hedonist case.

Hedonism has been considered because it illustrates the attempt to explain away 'goodness' in the ethical sense (or moral obligation) in terms of something else. There are other 'reductionist' theories;[1] for example, that the sense of moral obligation is a sort of embellishment of biological drives, practical expediency, or historical necessity. Of such theories we can say that people are fully entitled to think what they please, as long as they are consistent. If indeed the sense of moral obligation is nothing but a sophisticated form of animal instinct, or an attitude shaped by 'social pressures', let us give up using unnecessary terms such as 'ought', 'goodness', 'moral obligation', and the rest. And let us explain as best we can how it came to pass that mankind invented such sententious names for things that do not exist and which, being non-existent, could not have been experienced.

Most people would agree that it makes most sense to accept the age-old view that ethical values ('ought', etc.) are *sui generis*, and not reducible to terms of anything else. It is a view that dates back at least to Plato, and in Hebrew thought to a good deal earlier. We will assume, therefore, that 'Good' in the ethical sense 'is a unique objective character which we intuitively apprehend as "ought to be", and "ought to be striven for"'.[2]

Let us once more remind ourselves that the word 'ought', like 'good', is ambiguous. In 'You ought to have your hair cut', or 'You ought to spray your rose-trees', the 'ought' is not the same as in 'You ought to tell the truth'. In the first examples the word is instrumental; it indicates a means to an end – tidy appearance, or better roses. But 'You ought to tell the truth' has intrinsic value; it means that truth is not optional but obligatory irrespective of convenience or personal feelings. If truthfulness is in any sense instrumental, it is instrumental to the kind of personal relations in which persons can respect and trust one another. It is instrumental in the same sense as St Paul's gifts of the Spirit. Which is to say

---

[1] Or theories of 'nothing but'.
[2] Olaf Stapledon: *Philosophy and Living*, p. 205.

that it is inseparable from, and intrinsic to, the ultimate meaning and purpose of living.

It is this ethical, or intrinsic, good that we are discussing. Or, to put it functionally rather than ontologically, we are examining the implications of statements in the form of 'This is what I ought to do'. And it has been suggested that, if the use of 'ought' is justified at all, it refers to something *sui generis* in the situation, not translatable into other terms. If we could reduce the statement 'This is what I ought to do' to the form of 'This action gives me pleasure', or 'This behaviour has been established by social pressure', we should be reducing value-judgements to factual statements. 'This action gives me pleasure' is factual in the same sense as 'I have a headache'. But 'I ought to do such-and-such' is a statement on a different plane.

What is ethically obligatory is certainly connected with factual matters, since ethical judgements must apply in situations which have time, place and circumstances. But the ethical judgements cannot be identified with factual statements. Ethical judgements include an essential component which is not factual in the ordinary sense at all. What is 'good' ethically – what I ought to do – may or may not be desired, may or may not be convenient, easy, difficult, embarrassing. In fact, the 'oughtness' has no *necessary* connection whatever with desirability or convenience – or even possibility.[1]

At this point in the argument the Utilitarian might attempt a comeback on the following lines. There must be some long-term connection between ethical values and human satisfaction. If the pursuit of virtue brings, not happiness, but misery, why present virtue as a good thing, and why pursue it?

The answer to that is to acknowledge that there is indeed a relation between ethical values and human satisfaction. But the Utilitarian has the relation the wrong way round. Virtue, or goodness, is not good because it brings satisfaction; it brings satisfaction (if it does so) because it is good. The point may be illustrated from another field. We would not say that a joke is funny because it makes us laugh. Rather, it makes us laugh (if it does so) because it is funny. The man sitting in the corner-seat, reading the *New Yorker* with a completely dead-pan expression, may for all we know be inwardly very much amused. Jokes sometimes make us laugh;

---

[1] As to possibility, it would be more accurate to say that the *good* is not always possible – in this imperfect world. The situation may be one that permits only a choice of evils. It has been well said that it is not always possible to do the *good*, but that it is always possible to do *right* (the right action being perhaps the lesser of evils). Since we ought to do the right thing, it can be said that what we ought to do is always possible.

sometimes they don't. But, if we laugh, we laugh because the joke is funny; it is not funny because we laugh. For, after all, we sometimes laugh at situations that are far from amusing.

Similarly, we may get satisfaction from things that are far from virtuous. In the long term, however, it is common human experience that the pursuit of virtue brings happiness – though the happiness may be of a kind very different from what is commonly recognized as pleasure. Anyway, the happiness is a by-product. Virtue is not good because it brings happiness; it brings happiness because it is good. Indeed, it is a great mistake to make happiness an end in itself; if we do so, it eludes us and we end in frustration. It has been well said: 'The pursuit of happiness was ever a most unhappy quest.' The happy people are not those who try to be happy, but those who lose themselves in something which they believe to be worth while, to which they can dedicate themselves regardless of their own personal convenience or safety: saints, martyrs, explorers, scientists, social workers. Some of these illustrate the paradox of personal fulfilment in spite of suffering. In other cases a life of selfless dedication did not involve suffering. But, either way, the work brought happiness because it was good; it was not good because it brought happiness.

If we recognize moral obligation ('oughtness') as a value distinct from the fact of satisfaction or dissatisfaction, we are recognizing something that cannot be reduced to terms of something else – such as pleasure, social utility, or evolutionary trends. The fallacy of all 'reductionist' theories is that they confuse genetic with ontological categories. It is possible to trace the historical development of ethical values. The anthropologist and the social historian can throw light on the development of these values. But the development of an attitude is one thing, and its *validity* is another. If that distinction is not maintained, we are saying: Whatever is, is right. The *fact* that we can account for a number of contemporary social attitudes tells us nothing about their goodness or badness.

We can learn a great deal about human institutions, manners and customs, by studying their development. The historical dimension is always valuable in judging human problems. But we must avoid confusion of thought. Not only must we keep the distinction between the genetic and the ontological, since failure to do so leads to saying that what is, is right. We must also avoid what may be called the fallacy of 'nothing but'. Having traced the growth of, say, moral customs from their primitive origins to their civilized forms, there is a temptation to say that the civilized form is nothing but a sophisticated version of the primitive form. There was at one time a fashion of disposing of mature religion by tracing it back to primitive cults, and then saying that there is nothing more in the mature form than in the primitive cult. Thus the Christian doctrine of Atonement could be reduced to a vicarious projection (Isa. liii) of primitive ceremonies for cleansing from infectious disease (Lev. xiii–xiv). Similarly, we could say that marriage is nothing but mating, a dinner-party nothing but eating. It is equally reasonable to reverse the interpretation, and to see the mature form as revealing the true meaning, and the primitive origins as the first dim gropings after something to be fully understood much later. Indeed, the mature form can often throw more light on the primitive than the primitive can on the mature. The nature of a thing, as Aristotle said, is what that thing has in it to become. The acorn is a potential oak tree; and it would be perverse, at the least, to see nothing in an oak tree but an acorn. The truth is that each (the mature and the primitive) illuminates the other. Those who have studied a mother-dog with her puppies will recognize that human motherhood can teach us something about whelping, and that whelping can teach us something about human motherhood – notably, how much of it is instinctive.

If we agree to regard ethical obligation ('oughtness') as something *sui generis* and irreducible, the question still remains: What things are obligatory? This question can refer to the great variety of manners and customs which are evolved to give expression to underlying values. In the present connection it is more important to ask what is the supreme or ultimate value – the *summum bonum* – from which all other forms of goodness derive. On this question there is room for difference of opinion. But there is a fair consensus in favour of the view that the basis of any satisfactory morality is the respect – reverence is not too strong a word – of one human being for another. Kant enshrined this view in the principle that we should always treat other persons as ends in themselves, and never use them as means. Most generally accepted morality can be brought under that principle. Lying, stealing, violence, sexual promiscuity – such things are wrong because they make use of other people as means instead of respecting them as ends.

Having said that much, we cannot stop at the relation between man and man. We share the world with animals; and it is generally accepted that we have obligations to them. We also share the world with trees and plants and inanimate things, for the care and responsible use of which we may reasonably (as the most intelligent beings on earth) be regarded as answerable.[1]

If man has responsibility – and few would deny that he is responsible at least to his fellow-men – it would seem arbitrary to restrict that responsibility. We would not restrict it to men of his own race and colour. Why,

[1] This is written in European Conservation Year, 1970. Not long ago someone said: 'Man is the filthiest animal on earth.'

then, should we restrict it to mankind in general? Is it not reasonable to say that man is responsible in all his contacts with the world around him? If it is wrong to exploit other men, cruelty to animals is also wrong, and so is waste and pollution of the environment in general.

To speak of responsibility implies, not only that we are responsible *for* something, but also *to* something. Kant's principle that other persons should be treated as ends and not used as means may be compared with St John's 'Beloved, let us love one another: for love is of God; and every one that loveth is born of God, and knoweth God. He that loveth not knoweth not God; for God is love' (1 John iv. 7).

At this stage the argument is bound to move into the religious field – not necessarily in the sense of any specific theology, but in the sense of recognizing that the universe is not merely a chapter of accidents, but has coherence and meaning in which our own existences have meaning. That is to say, there must be some kind of Reality, in which we live and move and have our being, and to which we are answerable.

Another, and better, name for the proper reverence of person for person is love – in the sense of ἀγάπη, the brotherly love of the New Testament, which is neither sentimental nor possessive, but is a sincere striving for the welfare of others. Directly we think of love as the ideal relation between people, we come up against a dilemma. We cannot love to order. How can we love those whom we do not like? Indeed, the very words: 'I *ought* to love my neighbour' are a confession that I do not love him; for, if I did, there would be no need to impose the obligation.

There is a possibility of liberation from this contradiction of moral necessity; and it lies in the belief that, before we love, we are already loved. Love needs to be evoked, as is clear from the behaviour of infants. Love is initially a *response* to the Love that sustains us and the rest of creation. The passage quoted above from St John continues: 'Herein is love, not that we loved God, but that he loved us ... If God so loved us, we ought also to love one another' (1 John iv. 10, 11). We can love one another *in* God. Without some such faith in the ultimate goodness of the Reality in which our lives are grounded, it is hard to see how the most admirable ideals of universal fraternity can hope to get off the ground.

There remains the question how we *validate* ethical beliefs. What kind of 'proof' is appropriate to the sort of propositions that have been canvassed in the last few paragraphs?

We saw earlier that truth of fact is established by empirical evidence 'beyond all reasonable doubt'. Obviously we cannot apply that method to statements like 'I ought to love my neighbour' or 'God is Love'. Does it follow, therefore, that such statements are merely, so to say, exclamatory, and that we have no business to ask whether or not they are 'true'?

We may approach the answer by reflecting that the human mind needs not only a number of disparate pieces of knowledge or experience, but also a total, coherent view of life, in which I and all my objects of experience have to find their place. It is not suggested that everyone's total view of life is explicitly thought-out and articulated. Such systematic thinking-out is, or used to be, the special job of the philosopher. But each man is his own philosopher to the extent that he cannot rest until he feels that his world is of a piece, that it makes sense, with himself as part of it. Things that won't fit in, that defy explanation, are a worry until they have been accounted for. Our unresolved problems may range from anxiety about the population explosion, or the future of East–West relations, to something comparatively comfortable like U.F.O.s or the Loch Ness Monster. But, one way or another, we demand that our world be coherent. And we know too that we are cheating if we purchase coherence at the price of excluding what won't fit in. The puppy who tells himself: 'There is no cat' is purchasing only ephemeral immunity.

Here, then, is our criterion for truth of value. We judge whether or not to believe that we have freedom of choice, that God is Love, that we grow by giving rather than by getting, according to whether or not these and other beliefs make sense of life as we know it. In the field of values there is no 'proof' which is coercive in the way that a laboratory experiment, or a statistical demonstration, is coercive. That does not mean that truths of value are less important than factual truths; they may be far more important. The way in which to establish a truth of value is to draw out its implications and relate them to a total view of life. That proposition is most 'true' which makes most sense of most things. It is to be noted that the coherence and the totality of our interpretation of experience are equally important. We must ask, not only: 'Does this fit?', but: 'Have I left anything out?'

It has just been said that, in this field, there are no coercive proofs – except in so far as the weight of total and coherent good sense is coercive. We are at liberty, for example, to deny free will. But, if we decide to be strict determinists, we must submit to the same test of consistence. We must never act as if we had choice; and we must recognize that our belief in determinism is determined, not chosen. We are equally at liberty to be atheists, provided we satisfy ourselves that atheism gives us as coherent, as whole, and as meaningful an interpretation of experience as theism. Atheism is indeed a respectable intellectual position, provided one has made sure that one is adopting atheism for its positive merits and not as an escape from the more difficult problems of theism (such as the problem of evil).

What has been said in this chapter about ethical values and moral obligation clearly has educational bearings, some of which have been considered in earlier chapters. It will be convenient, however, to gather together the main conclusions.

A new interest in moral education has been aroused in recent years – partly because of the disturbance of moral standards and the spread of 'permissiveness' in the West, and partly because of a loss of confidence in religious education as a means of regulating conduct. In the last few years a good deal of attention has been given to the study and planning of moral education, either without any religious presuppositions, or on the basis of common ground between Christians and humanists.

One of the first important publications of this kind was sponsored by the Farmington Trust – *Introduction to Moral Education*, by John Wilson, Norman Williams and Barry Sugarman (Pelican, 1967). The authors are respectively a philosopher, a psychologist and a sociologist. This 450-page book is concerned with three main questions: (*a*) What is moral education, and who can be said to be morally educated?; (*b*) Which findings of psychology and social science are relevant to it?; (*c*) How can children be morally educated? There is much careful dissection of meaning, and the authors are seeking a rigorous methodology in their particular field. There is some useful advice to teachers; but the book is essentially a pioneer exploration. It is to be hoped that, on their next voyage, the crew will include a professional theologian. The least satisfactory part of the book is the brief passage on the relation between religion and moral education.

A more recent contribution in this field consists of two books (1969) by Dr N. J. Bull. One of these records a three-years' study of the development of moral judgement in 360 boys and girls ranging in age from seven to seventeen; and also considers the relation of moral judgement to intelligence (apparently the most significant factor), socio-economic class (less significant, but more so with boys than girls, i.e. boys seem to be more dependent on external authority), and religious class (i.e. church affiliation, which appears to be the least significant factor). Dr Bull's other book is shorter, and intended for teachers and students who may not have time to read the larger study. In it he summarizes his research, and examines the nature of moral judgement and the stages of its development.[1]

One of Dr Bull's most valuable chapters is on the relation between

[1] Norman J. Bull: *Moral Judgement from Childhood to Adolescence*; and *Moral Education* (Routledge and Kegan Paul), 1969.

morality and religion. This is a matter to be discussed in Chapter 7. For the moment it may be noted that Dr Bull's view, supported by considerable study, is that morality needs the support of religion, but that there are dangers in tying religion and morality too tightly together, lest the collapse of religion should bring morality down with it.

What follows is a summary of suggestions made about moral education in earlier chapters.

In the first place, the principle of 'learning by doing' applies *par excellence* in this field. The acceptance of moral principles is no guarantee of corresponding conduct. The moral education of the young can be helped by instruction and discussion; but it depends much more on the atmosphere of the school, co-operation between home and school, the example of teachers and other grown-ups. Schools in these days are far more out-going than they used to be. It is not unusual for schools to provide opportunity to study local government in action, see local industries at close quarters, and do some practical social service. In these ways boys and girls may learn the meaning of social relations, and of democracy: that democracy is something more than counting votes, and that the quality of a community is the quality of the people who belong to it rather than its form of government. The importance of personal quality in public life can be emphasized by the reading of biographies: a good way of extending one's knowledge of human nature and the next best thing to meeting the people themselves.

One of the most important lessons to be learnt, through experience and example, is that we grow as people through our relations with other people, and – still more important – that we grow by giving rather than by getting. We may or may not care to use the word 'love' in its New Testament sense. In English we suffer from having this one name for some very different things; and the word has been hopelessly sentimentalized and degraded. We may prefer to use some weaker word like 'fellowship'. However that may be, we have to remember that the most important thing in human life is the respect of person for person, the responsibility of persons to and for other persons. And we should not forget that the ἀγάπη of the New Testament is no sentimental attitude. It does not necessarily mean giving people what they think they want, it does not mean peace at any price, it does not necessarily mean being nice to people. It means sincerely seeking the real good of others, and using our brains to think out as well as we can what that real good is. Together with one's responsibility to others is one's responsibility to make the best one can of oneself. At the end of the day one is answerable for what one has become as well as for what one has done; and one is never entitled to say: 'I can do what I like with my own life. If I choose to do something which is bad for my health, if I choose to waste my abilities, that is nobody's business but mine.'

These reflections on self-discipline are a reminder that freedom and authority are not necessarily opposed to each other. True freedom means understanding the law of one's being, making that law one's own, and ordering one's life by that law. In that sense freedom is the recognition of necessity. *Per contra*, permissiveness is not freedom; it leads only to frustration, the erosion of meaning, and boredom. All undisciplined indulgence defeats itself.

An important part of moral education – and one that becomes increasingly important in a rapidly changing world, where different races, languages and customs are being brought together – is to learn to distinguish between underlying principles and the varied expressions of those principles in codes of conduct. People, and groups of people, often take offence at one another because of speech or behaviour which are quite superficial. Differences of class (the great gulf between U and non-U), or of race (strange eating habits, perhaps) may separate people whose basic values are, if not the same, at least reconcilable. In whatever social situations we find ourselves, we should seek such common ground as we have with others before taking offence at the differences. Apparently opposite manners and customs may be different ways of expressing the same underlying value. To take a trivial example, there are peoples among whom it is bad manners to talk at meals; whereas we are taught that it is polite to make conversation. In both cases the underlying principle is that respect should be shown to the host and his hospitality. At a more serious level, we can learn a great deal by reading some anthropology and comparative religion. In the words of Dr A. C. Bouquet: 'Taboos, sacrificial ceremonies and myths are the religious toys and models which are played with by the race in its childhood, but which are not idle things, since they prepare it for the more serious business of adult spiritual life, just as the bricks and dolls of boys and girls prepare them for handicraft and motherhood. No useful purpose can be served by treating "the sacraments of simple folk" with contempt.'[1]

Finally, it should be noticed that, although it is convenient to distinguish different aspects or areas of human activity (e.g. to distinguish cognitive, affective and conative activity, to distinguish statements of fact from judgements of value), human beings do not function in water-tight compartments. No mental activity is purely cognitive, purely affective, or purely conative, though one or the other may dominate. There is much less difference than might be supposed between scientific thinking and moral thinking. Science involves intuition and imagination, and personal

[1] A. C. Bouquet: *Comparative Religion* (Penguin).

participation, as was pointed out earlier.[1] Value-judgements involve factual matters. Ethics and religion involve logical processes. In all mental activity, the whole person is involved, whether in scientific investigation, artistic creation, or spiritual experience.

BIBLIOGRAPHY

AYER, A. J., *The Problem of Knowledge* (Penguin, 1956).
BANTOCK, G. H., *Education and Values* (Faber and Faber, 1965).
BULL, N. J., *Moral Judgement from Childhood to Adolescence* (Routledge and Kegan Paul, 1969).
BULL, N. J., *Moral Education* (Routledge and Kegan Paul, 1969).
DURKHEIM, E., *Moral Education* (Free Press, Glencoe, 1961).
EPPEL, E. M. and M., *Adolescents and Morality* (Routledge and Kegan Paul, 1966).
EWING, A. C., *Ethics* (English Univ. Press, 1953).
KAY, W., *Moral Development* (Allen and Unwin, 1968).
MONTEFIORE, A., *A Modern Introduction to Moral Philosophy* (Routledge and Kegan Paul, 1958).
PEI, M., *Words in Sheep's Clothing* (Allen and Unwin, 1970).
PETERS, R. S., *Ethics and Education* (Allen and Unwin, 1966).
PIAGET, J., *The Moral Judgement of the Child* (Routledge and Kegan Paul, 1932; 4th Impression 1965).
REID, L. A., *Ways of Knowledge and Experience* (Allen and Unwin, 1961).
REID, L. A., *Philosophy and Education* (Heinemann, 1962).
SCHEFFLER, I., *Conditions of Knowledge* (Scott, Foreman and Co., 1965).
TOULMIN, S., *The Place of Reason in Ethics* (C.U.P., 1950).
TOULMIN, S., *The Place of Ethics in Education* (C.U.P., 1953).
WILKES, K., *Religion and the Sciences* (R.E.P., 1969).
WILSON, J., et al., *Introduction to Moral Education* (Penguin, 1968).
WOOZLEY, A. D., *Theory of Knowledge* (Hutchinson, 1949).

[1] See an elaboration of this theme in Michael Polanyi: *Personal Knowledge* (Routledge and Kegan Paul)

Chapter 7
Morality and Religion

In these days when all our basic values are open to question, it is difficult to imagine a society in which morality and religion were taken for granted – not, of course, in the sense that people were consistently moral and religious, but in the sense that established codes and beliefs were accepted as true, and honoured, if only in the breach. Yet, if we look at the whole stretch of civilized history, we shall recognize that our modern disturbance of values is something very recent. Anyone born about 1900 will remember that, whatever conflicts children might have had with their parents, they still took for granted that, as they grew up, they would, broadly speaking, accept and assume their parents' values and codes of conduct. There have, of course, been changes down the centuries. There have been ages of faith and of doubt. There have been ages of strict behaviour and ages of licence. And there have always been groups of heretics and eccentrics. But it is doubtful whether, since modern Europe began to take shape in the Middle Ages, there has been such wide and deep disturbance of traditional values as came with the two World Wars of this century.

Today there is probably more concern (and uncertainty) about the education of the young in morality and religion than at any other time in our history. The purpose of this chapter is to examine the relations between religion and morality.

In ancient times, and among primitive peoples today, tradition is very powerful. Long-established laws and customs are sacred. Change is suspect. In such a form of society it is, for practical purposes, quite unnecessary to inquire into the truth of religious belief or to explore the grounds of moral obligation. These things come to be questioned only when their authority is shaken.

A good example of ancient, traditional morality and religion is the Hebrew Law, or *torah*. 'Torah' means 'instruction', and it was an essential feature of the Hebrew tradition that this instruction came from their God, Jahweh. It is worth noting that, in other oriental codes, such as the Sumerian, there is less emphasis on the divine source of the laws; it is the king, rather than the various deities, whose authority authenticates the law. But it has to be remembered that kings were at least semi-divine, and that these other eastern religions were polytheistic.

It is impossible to date the origin of the Hebrew Law. Substantially it may well belong to the time of Moses, and was gathered together during the early Monarchy. The Deuteronomic recodification was about 620 BC. The important thing is that the Jews were never concerned to change their Law, but only to make sure that they had a correct version of it. National disasters were the result of failure to keep the Law.

In later centuries, down to the time of Christ, there was detailed elaboration of the Law, not to change it, but to safeguard it from change. Unwritten legal decisions were incorporated. And the Scribes, professional students of the Law, hedged it about with rules (such as the thirty-nine actions prohibited on the Sabbath) which made the Law the formalistic monstrosity which Jesus so vigorously criticized. By the time of Christ the Pharisees and other strict Jews were in danger of being more concerned with correct ceremonial than with moral principles, and of thinking that a multitude of required actions added up to righteousness. It is, however, a mistake to condemn all Pharisees. There is a passage in the Talmud which gives seven classes of Pharisees, one of which kept the Law for its own sake and for the love of God, while the other six were self-righteous ceremonialists.

It is a far cry from the world of ancient Israel to the world of today, when both traditional morality and traditional religion are radically questioned.

In a BBC programme entitled, *The Question Why*,[1] conducted by Malcolm Muggeridge, the latest American moon project was discussed. It was pointed out that this enterprise had spotlighted the question whether, in our civilization, we had got our values right or wrong. Our civilization may be nearer catastrophe than we think. If it crashes, the disaster will not be due to lack of intelligence or of knowledge, but to our having wrong moral priorities. It so happened that on the same day Dr Frank Fraser Darling, in a Reith Lecture, said: 'Technology is apt to condition us psychologically so that man becomes its servant ... Technology is not of nature but of man, and is becoming the new god to which man seems inclined to relinquish his power of free will.'

Technology has come in for more than its fair share of adulation and of blame. In itself it is neutral. The future of civilization depends, not on how much knowledge man possesses, but on how he uses the knowledge he has. There are, nevertheless, obvious dangers in sudden bursts of scientific progress. The Encyclopaedists, on the eve of the French Revolution, thought that human reason and knowledge could produce the perfect society. And today we are open to the same temptation to think that traditional morality and religion are out of date.

[1] November 23, 1969.

The 'New Morality' of the permissive society, and the 'New Theology', popularized in this country by the ex-Bishop of Woolwich, are both so muddled that they cannot be simply expounded.[1]

There can be no doubt of the fact that, in the Western countries at least, there is a marked trend towards permissiveness in moral attitudes and conduct. There are various symptoms of this trend: an increase in crimes of violence, and of violent demonstrations, the relaxation of censorship and the presentation of crime, violence and sexual activity on stage and screen, the increase of drug addiction, especially among the young.

If we try to account for this trend to permissiveness, several factors can be distinguished. Technology, and scientific progress in general, have so altered the form in which moral problems present themselves that the traditional answers seem to become irrelevant, and people are confused as to what the problem really is. To take a very simple example: in days gone by it was customary to use the fear of pregnancy to reinforce sexual morality. Now that it is comparatively easy to sin in safety, it is natural to ask whether what used to be sin is, in fact, sin any more.

There is a great deal of muddled thinking among people who, by virtue of their education, might be expected to be clearer in their minds. There is muddle about sex, about 'love', 'peace', 'freedom', and many other important and emotive words. There is also confusion (due perhaps more to lack of knowledge than to muddled thinking) about such things as health and disease, drugs, pollution, and, in general, the side-effects of recent discoveries.

Some apologists for permissiveness confuse compassion with tolerance, seeming to justify permissiveness by appealing to the undoubted fact that society today is more compassionate than it was twenty-five years ago; more is done for the sick, the aged, the needy, and the treatment of criminals and the insane is more humane. But it would be a great mistake to equate compassion with tolerance. Tolerance says: Live and let live; let the junky have his dope if he wants it. Active compassion works for prevention and cure.

Although moral authority does not *necessarily* derive from religion, there is no doubt that morality and religion have in the past been tied together in such a way that the weakening of religious authority has brought with it a relaxation of moral codes. We may not have been brought up, like the ancient Israelites, to think of moral conduct in terms of Divine Command. But many now living were told as small children that God, or Jesus, would not love them if they were naughty; and the morality of the nursery was reinforced by hearing the Commandments

[1] See Chapters 2 and 3 of my *Religion and Morality* (R.E.P., 1967).

read in church. There is, as I shall try to show later in this chapter, a very real and valid connection between religion and morality; but it is to be found in the positive spirit of Jesus' teaching rather than in the negative teaching of 'Thou shalt not ...'. Unfortunately, religion as a social influence has been a restraint rather than an inspiration. It is the restraint that is now weakened, with the result that people – especially young people – go galloping out into what they believe to be freedom.

The greater independence and comparative affluence of teenagers is another factor in the encouragement of permissiveness. Teenagers, because they have money to spend and have not yet got fixed tastes, afford the advertiser a splendid market – for strange clothes, cigarettes, musical instruments, and more dubious commodities. It would, however, be wrong to hold teenagers responsible for a decline in moral standards. Their parents, who too often do not know their own minds, are as much to blame. And, throughout the affluent society, there is more leisure than most people know how to use. Affluence has gone to the affluent society's head. Reference was made in an earlier chapter to a television interview with residents on a caravan site which had been without electricity for several days. Almost without exception the people interviewed complained: 'The telly doesn't work. So there's nothing to do in the evenings.'

It has been pointed out by several recent writers[1] that the context of violence has been changing. Nuclear weapons reduce international conflict to the level of small wars and competitive deterrence. But social revolution is very much in fashion; conflicts are between classes, races, ideologies. The trend seems to be towards more violence within national states – not only criminal but increasingly political. The protest march is no new thing in history. But it now threatens to become a normal method of political influence. And it is to be noted that 'violence' is a very amenable word. Whatever you and your group may do is 'non-violent'. But anything which your opponents do to restrain you is 'violent'.[2] It is wise to remember that violence can be psychological as well as physical; and that the human spirit can be crushed without leaving any bruises on the body.

If we now attempt a critique of the trend to permissiveness, several observations may be made. In the first place, permissiveness is not freedom, nor the gateway to freedom. It leads progressively to erosion of meaning, frustration, and ultimate boredom. We can repeat four-letter words until

---

[1] See, for example, Hannah Arendt: *On Violence* (Allen Lane, 1970); and Jacques Ellul: *Violence* (S.C.M. Press, 1970).

[2] A real gem was produced several times early in July, 1970, by an Irish politician who asked our sympathy for 'people exposed to attack by the forces of law and order'.

they mean no more than the indefinite article. We can look at nudity until it moves us no more than the plucked poultry on a butcher's slab. The greatest danger of permissiveness, perhaps, is not the corruption of the human mind but its literal an-nihil-ation. It is a sobering thought that our civilization, if it is not destroyed by nuclear explosion, or by pollution, might be destroyed by boredom. If faced with the prospect of being bored to extinction, many of us would prefer to be blown to pieces.

Secondly, it must be conceded that people cannot be made good by legislation. Only education can make people better – and even the beneficent influence of education may have its limits. To say that people cannot be improved by law does not mean that legislation has no useful place in supporting the morality of a civilized people. What it does mean is that no law has ever been successfully enforced which did not have the substantial backing of public opinion. But law and regulation (e.g. censorship) may be useful in expressing a people's standards of values, and in restraining the minority who need control. Law is a reminder to the many, and a restraint upon the few.

Thirdly, the first step towards the establishment of a firm moral foundation is to be able to distinguish between those moral standards that can and do change and those which, if valid at all, are valid everywhere and at all times. It is salutary to remind ourselves, now and then, of the extent to which standards do change. Miss Henrietta Bowdler, sister of the famous Dr Bowdler, always closed her eyes at the Opera if any dancing took place, because dancing was so indelicate. It is hard for us to enter into Miss Bowdler's point of view.

The aim of moral education should be to seek, and make explicit, the principles underlying codes of conduct. Problems of sex morality, for example, must be seen and judged in the light of the unchanging principle of reverence between human beings as such. This basic principle will not answer every question about sexual morality. It will not provide a coin-in-the-slot answer to the question whether sexual intercourse outside marriage is always wrong. But it will provide a background against which these questions have some chance of being seen in their right perspective. The traditional rule of chastity outside marriage and fidelity within it can at least be looked at from the standpoint of that basic principle of human relations. Is a unique partnership likely to have more meaning and value than looser liaisons? Again, if we consider drug-taking, let us remember that we are responsible not only for what we do to other people, but also for what we make of ourselves.

Something was said in Chapter 6 about the grounds of morality: in particular, the need to examine the basic principles underlying codes of behaviour. An essential characteristic of Jesus' teaching was his constant appeal from the letter of the law to the spirit behind the law. The Pharisees and doctors of the Law, who thought more of ceremonial than of kindness and mercy, incurred his condemnation. The letter killeth; the spirit giveth life. That does not mean – as the permissivists would sometimes have us think – that our actions do not matter, provided we do not actively annoy people. The ethic of Jesus was immensely more rigorous and astringent than the comfortable tolerance of Flower People, or whatever may be their up-to-date equivalent. The 'love' of the New Testament is something very different from mere tolerance. The ethic of Jesus was radically uncompromising. It was, in mundane terms, an impossible ethic. That is why, through the centuries, we make a continual mess of it and yet we can never escape its claim upon us. It is a radical ethic, because it lays bare the motives behind our actions. The evil desire is as ungodly as the evil deed. We may not have murdered anybody, nor committed adultery; but we may be guilty in our hearts. And God sees into the heart. And, once we have seen our own hearts as God sees them, we cannot be comfortable.

> Came on the following Feet,
> And a Voice above their beat –
>   'Naught shelters thee, who wilt not shelter Me.'
>
> Halts by me that footfall.
> Is my gloom, after all,
> Shade of His hand, outstretched caressingly?
>   'Ah, fondest, blindest, weakest,
>   I am He whom thou seekest!
> Thou dravest love from thee, who dravest Me.'[1]

To end this part of the discussion on a more frivolous note: the correspondence columns of the *Sunday Telegraph* for December 7, 1969, contained the following brief excursion into futurism by one reader:

'I had just returned from an ESP trip to 1984 when I read Mr Duff Hart-Davis's interesting article in your issue of November 30 on the Sexual Revolution. Unfortunately I cannot offer much hope to all those who are now romping into the New Freedom. I found that, by 1984, sex had become the world's almighty, crashing bore, compared with which the misery of compulsory protest demonstrations was a picnic.

'The more puritanical citizens of 1984 were still grimly persisting in their duty to enrich their personalities by regularly sleeping with at least five partners. This was Required Behaviour under the Code of the

---

[1] Francis Thompson: *The Hound of Heaven.*

National Mental Health Service; and I gathered that the penalty for non-observance was very nasty. Even so, I had the impression that the less conscientious were getting away with a good deal of sex-evasion. An aged anthropologist confided to me his opinion that the ancient notion that sex was sinful arose from a primitive intuition that this is just how it would all end.

'In spite of tremendous official pressure, there were signs in 1984 of dangerous heresy and deviant behaviour among teenagers, whose attitudes were a matter of growing concern to their elders. I gathered that some (known as Mogams) were trying to revive an old and evil practice known as "going steady", which involved an unbalanced concentration on one partner. It was whispered that a strange secret sect had been formed, whose members practised a form of psychic self-mutilation called Chastity.

'You will understand, Sir, that my technique of ESP time-travel is still only experimental, and I was not able to stay in 1984 very long. I shall hope to report more fully on later occasions.'

Before discussing the New Theology, some attempt should be made to state, as simply as possible, the old theology, that is, the enduring essentials of the Christian faith. This is not an easy task. It is one that I have tried to tackle on several occasions from 1946 onwards. Readers will perhaps forgive me if I now make use of some passages from *Religion and Morality* (1967).[1]

The Christian Gospel is an answer to the human problem; and the first thing, therefore, is to define that problem: 'Man is a self-contradictory creature, at odds with himself, who cannot make a success of himself at the "natural" or animal level, but continually falls down in the attempt to attain "higher" goals. As St Paul put it, "The good that I would I do not, and the evil that I would not, that I do." This contradiction is the source of the great gulf between man and the other animals, which are far more perfect of their kind than man is, and who, in Walt Whitman's words, "are so placid and self-contained ... They do not sweat and whine about their condition; they do not lie awake in the dark and weep for their sins; they do not make me sick discussing their duty to God."

'This contradictoriness of man's nature, his perpetual frustration and divine discontent, is the most important fact about him, and the source not only of his despair but of his creative achievements. Without it he would have no art, no science, no philosophy, no history. Throughout his history (which offers little encouragement to a belief in human perfectibility) he is haunted by the ultimate questions about his own nature, whether there is any deliverance from ultimate frustration, whether there

---

[1] *Religion and Morality* (R.E.P., 1967), pp. 18–21; quoted by kind permission of the publishers.

is any valid attitude to life but Stoic resignation or irresponsible hedonism. The problem is dramatically presented by the Existentialists – for example in Albert Camus' *The Myth of Sisyphus*, whom the Gods had condemned to struggle ceaselessly to push a rock to the top of a mountain, whence it fell back of its own weight ... In Greek mythology opinions differ as to the reason for Sisyphus' punishment. But all versions agree that he had, like Prometheus, stolen the secrets of the Gods. He is the tragic hero, who reaches to heaven and is cast into hell.

'The answer of Christian theology to the human problem is a daring one. It boldly takes the baffling mystery of man's self-contradictory nature and makes it explain everything else, so that out of the darkness the light shines.

'Man is made in God's image. That is to say, he is not only creature, along with the other animals, but also creator. He not only experiences; he constructs authoritative comments upon his experience, in art, science and philosophy. That is man's freedom ...

'In reaching for the stars man forgets his natural limitations. As creator, he rebels against his creatureliness. Not content to bear the image of God, he wants to *be* God, to grasp and dispose of his own destiny, to seize, like Prometheus, the fire from heaven.

'It is thus that man runs his head into frustration. The rebellion against his creatureliness, which the Greek dramatists knew as the pride which is overtaken by doom, is what the theologians call "sin". It is significant that sin is not the outbreak of a lower side of man's nature, but the corruption of the best in him. That is why he cannot rescue himself from his predicament, but needs what the theologians call "redemption".

'It is the love of God that can rescue man from the ultimate tragedy which, however noble, is nevertheless his ruin. Redemptive love is not coercive, and therefore does not take away freedom. Man can always resist God's saving love.

'To save, God in Christ enters the world's pain and overcomes evil in the only way that evil can be finally overcome – by undergoing it. There is nothing *outré* or unearthly about this doctrine; for we know in homely experience that love alone gives freedom (it is less trouble to withhold freedom), and only love can redeem the misuse of freedom.

'Christian theology thus takes the facts of human life and history seriously (the central fact being man's inability to perfect himself by his own powers and resources), makes sense of them, and offers an answer which, though cosmic in scale, nevertheless conforms to homely experience as Newton's theory of gravitation conformed to the fall of the apple.

'The obligation to love one another stems from God's loving purpose in creating us in freedom, which confers on each human being his intrinsic worth. If Christ died for me, He died for my friends, my enemies, and the millions of whom I know nothing. We are brothers because we are children of God.'

Brief and inadequate as this summary is, it may provide a background against which we can look at some of the questions raised by the 'New Theology'.

It was in 1963 that Dr John Robinson, then Bishop of Woolwich, published his best-seller, *Honest to God*. Before that, few people outside the ranks of theological scholarship knew much about the New Theology, or had paid much attention to the writings of Tillich, Bonhoeffer and Bultmann. It might have been better had Dr Robinson got his own ideas clearer before sharing them with the public. But, on balance, it is probably a good thing that, by writing his book, he forced a fairly wide reading public to take notice of what has come to be known loosely as the New Theology. The name is perhaps unfortunate. For the best of the New Theology is not new.

Nobody could doubt Dr Robinson's honesty. But there is a certain amount of woolliness in *Honest to God*. We can go along with the rejection of a God 'up there' or 'out there'. But how much better off are we with a God 'in the depths' (of what?) or as 'the ground of being' (Tillich)? Something will be said later about Tillich. For the moment, although it would be wrong to suggest that his phrase 'the ground of being' does not convey meaning, it is as well to note the obscurity of such statements as: 'The centre of our whole being is involved in the centre of all being; and the centre of all being rests in the centre of our being.'

It is not easy to disentangle Dr Robinson's own thought. On the one hand he clearly says that the statement 'God is Love' cannot properly be reversed into 'Love is God'. Yet at other times he comes near to saying that the only way in which we can know Christ is in the love of our fellow men.

There are some helpful, and some less helpful, elements in the New Theology. We are in Professor Tillich's debt – and perhaps even more in debt to Dr W. R. Matthews, lately Dean of St Paul's – for insisting on dynamic rather than static categories in Christology.

One of the difficulties about Christian theology is in the difference between Hebrew and Greek modes of thought. Early Christian theology was thought and formulated in Greek terms, and was metaphysical and logical. Thus the Council of Chalcedon stated that Christ is truly God and truly man, 'of one substance with the Father as touching his godhead, and the same of one substance with us as touching his manhood, sin alone excepted', two natures in one person. The New Testament writers, however, who were cradled in the Hebrew Scriptures, were not interested in natures and substance. Hebrew thought was historical rather than metaphysical. And New Testament theology was functional rather than logical.

Tillich recalls us to Hebrew and New Testament ways of thinking when he pleads for a dynamic theology. The Hebrew prophets were concerned, not with what God *is* but with what he *does*. So was Jesus himself. And so was St Paul. We are truer to the New Testament, and more intelligible to our own contemporaries, if we say that in Jesus God was manifestly active, rather than that Jesus has a 'divine nature' or that he is 'of one substance with the Father'. Tillich suggests that we should replace the concept 'divine nature' by the concepts 'eternal God-man-unity' or 'eternal God-Manhood'. Such concepts, in his own words, 'replace a static essence by a dynamic relation'. St Paul's 'Christ the image of the invisible God' conveys the heart of the matter.

On the other hand, it is open to question how helpful Tillich is when he asks us to think of God as the 'ground of being'. Certainly there is danger in thinking of God as *a* person, distinct from ourselves and his universe. And there is meaning in identifying God with Being itself, or thinking of Him as the Creative Spirit in all Being. But equally there are dangers in abstraction. Anthropomorphism and abstraction are the Scylla and Charybdis of theology. There is always the risk that, in getting away from anthropomorphism, we become abstract and finish up with something, not more than personal, but less than personal. All our attempts to imagine God must be inadequate. But at least God must be Personal in the sense that he meets all the needs of our own personalities, for communication and response. It would indeed be quite unfair to Tillich to suggest that he believed otherwise. Although much of what Tillich says is difficult to follow, he writes quite positively of a 'person-to-person encounter with God'. When he speaks of God as the 'depth and ground of all being', he means not only that God is the source of all being, but that God is our ultimate concern – what we take seriously without reservation. And he makes the point that, if God *is* ultimate reality, there can be no sense in asking whether God exists! That is to say, God is not a presiding V.I.P. above, and distinguishable from, the rest of the universe. On the other hand, we might protest that Tillich is knocking on an open door; so far are we from quarrelling with him that no sensible person would think otherwise. And, as for God's involvement in His universe, the doctrine of the Incarnation makes that clear enough.

Dr Rudolf Bultmann's concern to 'demythologize' the New Testament is also somewhat doubtful as a source of illumination. Certainly the Bible is full of picture-language, much of which is no longer intelligible, and some of which could be a stumbling-block in our own day. Dr Bultmann has in mind such phrases as 'God sent his son' and 'He ascended into Heaven'. References to Christ's pre-existence, incarnation, ascent, descent, trouble Dr Bultmann, lest they should put modern man off the Gospel. There is certainly force in his view that imagery has no value when it has become petrified; we do not want a collection of theological fossils. On the other hand, it would not do modern man any harm to make the effort to understand the imagery of the Bible. If we strip the Gospel story of everything that lifts it above pedestrian historical narrative, we are in danger of throwing out the baby with the bath water.

Here we reach what, in the opinion of some, is the real trouble with Bultmann. As Professor Ninian Smart puts it,[1] Bultmann was so sceptical about the possibility of reconstructing the historical Jesus that his emphasis is wholly on an existential Christ. 'The trouble with this view is that it makes history irrelevant to the truth of Christianity. Provided the disciples, and Paul, had an experience of the risen Lord, it matters not who Jesus claimed to be or how he acted.' That is no doubt a legitimate view to take, but it is scarcely founded on the New Testament. The Christian faith is rooted in historical events in time.

Dietrich Bonhoeffer was a heroic martyr under Nazi persecution, and his private writings (in particular his prayer for fellow-prisoners) leave no room for doubt about his deep personal piety. The reality of his devotional life makes it the harder to understand his thesis that modern man has come of age and outgrown the need for a Father-God. When we reflect on his sufferings under Nazi power, we can see that even divine power may have become abhorrent to him. Christ's cry from the Cross, 'Why hast thou forsaken me?' may supply a clue to Bonhoeffer's thinking. Man must learn to share the loneliness of Christ, and in that sense do without God. Yet there are passages in Bonhoeffer's writings which seem to state, quite flatly, that a personal God is out of date, and that attempts to recall the world to a traditional Christianity are in fact a betrayal of Christianity.

If there is a common factor in the various exponents of the New Theology, it is the effort to make Christianity comprehensible to the modern mind. Theology in any age must be alive in the sense of reckoning with, and interpreting, the contemporary world. There is not likely to be agreement on the issues raised by the New Theology. Broadly speaking, there are three possibilities. One is that the New Theologians are right in believing (with Dr Robinson) that a revolution in theological thinking is necessary; otherwise Christian faith and practice will be abandoned. Another is that the New Theology at its best conveys to us something that we could get as well or better from intelligent study of the New Testament. In other words, the New Theologians are trying to save us

[1] *Secular Education and the Logic of Religion* (Faber).

from mistakes which sensible theologians have never made. A third view is that some of the New Theology may, with the best of intentions, turn Christianity into something else which is more acceptable to modern man, rather than educate modern man to understand Christianity. One aspect of this kind of transmutation is emphasized by Professor Jacques Ellul, who attacks the 'Man-come-of-age' and 'Death-of-God' theology as an attempt to identify Christianity with social revolution – or at least with social reform – by getting rid of the transcendental quality of Christianity. Not that Professor Ellul is against social justice or even revolutionary means of achieving it. But he is strongly against the kind of muddled or disingenuous thinking that would equate Christianity with social justice and/or revolution. He writes: 'The Christianity that accommodates itself to the culture in the belief that it will thus make itself more acceptable and better understood, and more authentically in touch with humanity – this is not a half-Christianity; it is a total denial of Christianity. Once Christianity gives way to accommodation or humanistic interpretation, the revelation is gone. Christian faith is radical, decisive like the very word of God, or else it is nothing.

'Now it is precisely a lack or a toning down of radicalism that characterizes the modern theological orientation (as it has so often characterized other theologies in the course of Church history). Paul Tillich's theory of culture, Rudolf Bultmann's demythologization, today's Death-of-God theology are all adaptations of Christianity to what is conceived of as the nature of man and modern society. It is very important for us to understand that every such effort, however intelligent, radically attacks the Lordship of Jesus Christ by removing its content and its power. This is not a matter of interpreting reality in a new way, giving it a new content, etc. Such accommodation robs the gospel of its radicalism and consequently renders the Christian powerless in the struggle against violence. To seek conciliation with the world is to cut off the gospel's roots.'[1]

Professor Ellul takes us to an extreme opposite to that which he attacks. Like Hobbes, he sees violence as the natural condition of human society. Every state is established by violence, which is then legitimized. He sees the Christian's duty in stark contrast with the world-order. The Christian is actively involved in the world, but, if he be true to his Christian allegiance, he must not use the world's weapons. He must witness to social injustice, speak for the oppressed, mediate between oppressed and oppressors, expose the world's evil by undergoing it.

In taking this uncompromising line, Professor Ellul strikes uncomfortably at the reader's conscience and poses one of the perpetual problems

[1] Jacques Ellul: *Violence* (S.C.M. Press, 1970), pp. 146–7.

of human history. One is left wondering, if all government begins and continues in violence, and violence breeds nothing but violence, how a state of law and order can ever be reached in which the arts of peace can flourish. Without the Roman Empire there could have been no Christendom. Does this mean that Christendom was historically possible only by compromising the faith of Christ? On that question Christians themselves are never likely to agree. But to pose the question is at least to remind us that we dwell in two interpenetrating worlds, of the ideal and the actual, the transcendental and the mundane, and that we are inescapably caught up in both. There is perhaps no logical answer to the question of the relation between them. But we must, in our living, work out some kind of pragmatic answer.

It remains to consider the relation between morality and religion, and between moral and religious education. The new concern about both moral and religious education is a sign of the times in which we live. And it is no less significant that opinion is sharply divided on the question of the relation between them. Some want moral education to be tightly connected with religious education. Others want to keep moral education separate from religion. At one extreme are those who believe that the only basis for morality is religious. At the other extreme are those who reject religion and have no use for transcendental authority in matters of conduct. There are also a good many middle-of-the-road people (both religious and agnostic) who see the danger of connecting morality and religion too closely together, lest the rejection of religion should carry with it the rejection of morality.

Clearly there can be morality without religion and religion without morality.[1] But it is impossible to study one without the other, because historically they have been inextricably involved with each other. Nor can either be taken for granted, in an age marked by the disintegration of traditional patterns of thought and belief. It is this disintegration of the traditional pattern of values, rather than any dramatic degeneration of behaviour, that necessitates a new effort to understand the nature of morality and religion and the relation between them.

Broadly speaking there are three possible views about the nature of morality and its relation with religion:

(1) At one extreme is the view that moral insight and conduct depend entirely on transcendental revelation and inspiration. Man can do nothing of himself. God commands and man must obey. This view, or an approximation to it, is recognizable in some extreme forms of Protestantism, and

---

[1] The point was humorously made in the remark: 'The problem in the Protestant countries is to make moral people religious, and in the Catholic countries to make religious people moral.'

in our time is characteristic of Karl Barth. Adherents of this view, confronted by the plain fact that many people live highly moral lives while rejecting all religious belief, take the line that the virtuous agnostic is living on the spiritual capital of past generations of believers; and it is certainly true that inherited habits of conduct may outlive the beliefs that once supported them.

This transcendental view of morality is open to criticism on two main grounds. In the first place, it implies a blanket condemnation of the natural sinfulness of all human things, which could imperil what Reinhold Niebuhr called the 'relative moral achievements of history'. Either there is something in the nature of man which is ready and able to respond to the saving Grace of God – which is, so to say, groping towards the light – or else it becomes impossible to explain how the Grace of God can find any soil in which to take root.

The other objection to this view of morality is the pragmatic one that transcendental authority may be claimed for imperfect, transient moral codes, in such a way that moral progress may be held back, rather than promoted, by religious faith. The pages of history are blotted with the sins of blindness and bigotry; and, in the words of Burke, 'religious persecution may shield itself under the guise of a mistaken and overzealous piety'.

(2) At the opposite extreme is the view that moral values have no supernatural connections whatever – that the supernatural is nothing but the figment of an immature or muddled imagination. The basis of morality is human reason, which tells us that the necessary condition of human happiness is the proper respect of one human being for another. The secular humanists rest their case on man's ability to perceive the good and pursue it. What need is there for thunder and lightning from Sinai when we have reason and common sense to guide us?

The trouble about this view is quite simply that it doesn't work. Men have always known that the world would be a better place if people behaved decently to one another. The problem is that, century by century and millennium by millennium, they don't do it. Today we have perhaps a million times the technological power over our environment that our predecessors only a century ago possessed. Yet twentieth-century man is still as much at the mercy of the seven deadly sins[1] as his ancestors five hundred, or five thousand, years ago. The optimism of the secular humanists has a certain naïve charm. It is a pity that historic human experience so woefully belies it.

(3) There is a third view, which we may call Christian Humanism. It is rooted in the New Testament, and comes to us *via* Augustine and

[1] Anger, lust, gluttony, sloth, pride, envy, avarice.

Thomas Aquinas. It has been notably restated in our own day by Jacques Maritain:

'I am well aware,' writes Maritain,[1] 'that to some an authentic humanism can by definition only be one that is anti-religious. I hold the contrary opinion ...

'Western humanism springs from religious and "transcendental" sources without which it would be incomprehensible even to itself. (I call "transcendental" all those forms of thought, however otherwise diverse, which find the principle of the world in a Spirit greater than man – in man a soul whose destiny is outside time – in a natural or supernatural piety the centre of our moral life.) The springs of Western humanism are classical and Christian; it is not only in the mass of medieval antiquity, but also in the most authentic part of the heritage of pagan antiquity, that which is evoked by the names of Homer and Sophocles, of Socrates and Virgil ... that we see these characteristics of which I have spoken. Again, by the very fact that the order of medieval Christendom was one of a unity of soul and flesh or of incarnate Spirit, it held in its consecrated form a virtual and implicit humanism ...'

He goes on to note the historical separation of modern humanism from its transcendental sources. 'Against this materialized spirituality, the active materialism of atheism and paganism has the game in its hands. But, sundered from their natural roots and set in a climate of violence, it is still in part Christian impulses gone astray, which in fact, existentially, move the hearts of men and rouse them into action. Is it not a sign of the confusion of ideas which today extends over the whole world that we see such one-time Christian impulses aiding the propaganda of cultural ideas which are diametrically opposed to Christianity? The time is ripe for Christians to bring things back to the fount of truth ... thus raising a cultural and temporal force of Christian inspiration able to act in history and come to the aid of men.

'This new humanism ... I see as directed towards a socio-temporal realization of that evangelical concern for humanity which ought not to exist only in the spiritual order, but to become incarnate; and towards the ideal of a true brotherhood among men.'

In terms of Christian humanism, truth and goodness are neither wholly transcendental nor wholly immanent, but both at once. The doctrine of the Fall is true; so also is it that we are made in the image of God. Human virtue is the response of the divine within ourselves to the divine beyond ourselves. Human nature is corrupt in the sense that every human being needs to be rescued from the corruption which is inseparable from the divine gift of creative freedom, that is, the temptation to be free *from*

[1] *True Humanism* (Bles, 1938), pp. xiv ff.

God rather than to be free *for* God: to claim self-sufficiency and thus usurp the place of God. On the other hand, Divine Redemption cannot work unless the human soul is able and ready to respond. There is nothing coercive about the Grace of God. Where human hearts resist him, Christ can do no mighty works.

This view, stated above in terms of Christian theology, can – as Maritain recognizes in the passage quoted – be more generally stated in terms of Platonic philosophy, which equally postulates the 'given' Reality, and the human capacity for response. The important difference between Christianity and Platonism – and indeed between Christianity and the other great religions of the world – is that, in Christian theology, God in Christ Himself enters the world's pain, frustration and failure, and overcomes the world's evil by undergoing it. In other words, God moves in to rescue man from a predicament from which he cannot extricate himself. By recognizing the ultimate tragedy of the purely human predicament, the Greek dramatists showed a deeper insight than the Greek philosophers. The insight of Greek tragedy is unsurpassed in profundity anywhere outside the New Testament. It is the Christian Gospel which, by turning the whole human situation upside-down, converts tragedy into triumph.

In the present context, however, we are primarily concerned with the dual interpretation of man's nature and destiny which is common to Platonism and Christianity. The bi-polarity, which we have constantly encountered in other connections, is here in its most fundamental form. On the one hand there is the worth of human reason and insight, raising man above the rest of the animal creation. On the other hand is the need for some kind of 'redemption' from beyond man's own human resources, without which the human condition, however noble, could end only in tragedy. This is the great paradox and conflict of the human condition, that man, though part of Nature, can never solve his problems – as other animals can – on the merely 'natural' level.

Within the terms of this third, bi-polar view of morality and religion, we can say that a purely humanistic (meaning, by that, an atheistic or agnostic) interpretation of morality is valid as far as it goes. It does not, however, go far enough; for it ends in the question-mark attached to the failure of man through the centuries to do what he knows perfectly well he ought to do and would benefit from doing. If reason and knowledge were sufficient, man should be nearer to fulfilment than ever before. Instead, we are talking seriously of a possible world catastrophe, material and moral.

The problem of the relation between morality and religion could be summed up by asking: Is there such a thing as Christian morality? And, if so, what is it?

The answer to the first question is both Yes and No, according to what is meant by 'Christian morality'. If 'Christian morality' is taken to mean a set of rules or commandments, deriving their authority solely from certain writings, then the answer is that there is no such Christian morality. The last thing that Jesus demanded was that people should live by the book. He broke through the letter to the Spirit within. One of his favourite teaching techniques was to leave his listeners with a problem on their minds, for which they must work out a solution. And he constantly appealed to the experience of life itself to reveal the truth; his teaching about God found its echo and confirmation in human relations and the human heart. It is important for Christians and non-Christians alike to recognize that the Christian Gospel reinforces moral standards that are indicated by reason and good sense. Christianity does not substitute a book of rules alien to the experience of mankind, nor insist on the goodness or badness of anything that would not be good or bad in any case.

If, on the other hand, we take 'Christian morality' to mean the Law of Love, then morality becomes central to the Gospel. 'He that doeth His will shall know of the teaching.' In that sense Christianity is essentially an ethical religion. Nothing in the New Testament is clearer than the uncompromising statement of the Law of Love, and the condemnation of man's exploitation of his fellow-men.

We are left with this question. If Christianity reinforces a morality that stands to reason, is Christianity really necessary? The last thing a professing Christian should do is to denigrate the qualities and achievements of enlightened agnostics, who may well enter the Kingdom of Heaven ahead of us. But perhaps the shortest and clearest way to the heart of the question is to consider St Paul's spiritual journey from 'bondage to the Law' to the freedom of his Christian discipleship.[1]

This transformation of St Paul's life was sketched in Chapter 3, where the paradox of freedom and authority was under consideration. Paul was a prisoner under the Law because the Law, while laying down what a man should do, does not give him the power to do it. But his new freedom of slavery to Christ had the warmth and enthusiasm of a personal loyalty, in comparison with which mundane misfortunes were of no account. 'Not I, but Christ in me.'

A good deal was said in Chapter 6 about moral education. A few further comments may be offered, on the relation between moral and religious education.

In the first place, we ought to be aware of the swing of emphasis in the

[1] The last three paragraphs are based on part of an article, 'Morality in a Permissive Society', in *The Modern Free Churchman*, summer, 1970.

past hundred years from personal to social morality. The new emphasis on social morality is all to the good inasmuch as it makes us more aware of the needs of people less fortunate than ourselves, and in other parts of the world. Unfortunately, it also invites the conclusion that personal morality no longer matters very much. What is a domestic indiscretion compared with a large-scale fiddle on the stock exchange or a war in the Far East? The truth is that personal morality matters as much as ever it did. If the basis of morality is the respect of one human being for another, then personal, or private, morality is quite as important as social, or public, morality. Earlier in this chapter some passages were quoted from Professor Ellul's book, *Violence*, in which he reminds us of the danger of letting the social conscience become a substitute for the personal conscience. That way lies the temptation of using the social conscience as a cloak for group interests. At the end of the day each individual must find himself alone with eternity. As A. N. Whitehead puts it: 'Religion is what the individual does with his own solitariness. It runs through three stages, if it evolves to its final satisfaction. It is the transition from God the void to God the enemy, and from God the enemy to God the companion.'[1]

When the case has been made out for moral education on its own merits, it is still true that a person is not educated who has not been brought into confrontation with the transcendental, supernatural, Divine, or whatever word is preferred. The practical question is whether man is, or can be, self-sufficient. Can he truthfully and realistically see himself as master of his fate as well as captain of his soul; or must he recognize that his creativeness is conditioned by his creatureliness? If he must indeed make that acknowledgement, then man's recognition of his creatureliness is the basic religious act, upon which the whole religious life is conditional.

It is not the purpose of this book to discuss religious education as such. But this chapter may conveniently end with two observations designed to avoid misunderstanding.

In the first place, in studying religion we should avoid the idea that religious feeling is, so to speak, the exercise of a distinct faculty. Religious truth is not a special or different *kind* of truth about life. Rather, if it is anything, it is the *whole* truth about life. Its totality is its distinguishing mark. Biology may concern itself with man's metabolism, sociology with his social relations. But when we think of man, as man, in all his aspects and relations, we are thinking about the things that religion and theology are concerned with.

Secondly, recent discussion of religious education has been bedevilled by some confusion about what is called 'indoctrination'. There are some

[1] A. N. Whitehead: *Religion in the Making*, Lowell Lectures, 1926.

who say that we ought not (in the State schools at any rate) to teach religion, but that we should only teach *about* religion. The implication is that 'teaching religion' means overriding the pupil's critical faculty and imposing a doctrine upon him, whereas 'teaching about religion' means putting the pupil in a position to make up his own mind.

We must of course concede at once that no teaching, whatever the subject, is good teaching if it overrides the pupil's responsible freedom of mind. A good practical distinction between education and propaganda is that education seeks to stimulate thought, while propaganda seeks to anaesthetize thought (while if possible deluding the victim into believing that he is thinking). No sensible person would attempt to justify religious teaching which came under this condemnation of discouraging, rather than stimulating, thought. A study of Jesus' own teaching methods will show that he used various techniques to make his hearers think for themselves. One of his favourite ways of dealing with people who asked him trick questions was to reply with a further question, which deepened the issue, and sent his hearers away with an awkward problem on their minds.

To say that all good religious teaching should make people think, rather than prevent them from thinking, is, however, a very different thing from saying that the teacher who 'teaches religion', as distinct from 'teaching about religion', is guilty of 'indoctrination'. There is no necessary contradiction between the positive presentation of what the teacher believes to be true, and his proper respect for the pupil's responsibility for doing his own thinking. The best teachers, whether they are teaching religion, music, history or science, combine these two functions. Nobody would say, for example, 'Don't teach music; only teach about music.'

Moreover, it has to be remembered that nothing can really be learnt without experiencing it as well as inspecting it. Whether the subject be religion, music, or even mathematics, it cannot be fully understood without being, as it were, felt from within, and not only observed from without. If 'teaching about religion' means the exclusion of experience (including experience of worship), then it is educational nonsense. Such limited teaching does not even equip the pupil to reject what he has been taught.

BIBLIOGRAPHY

ACLAND, R., *We Teach Them Wrong* (Victor Gollancz, 1963).
ALVES, C., *Religion and the Secondary School* (S.C.M. Press, 1968).
ARENDT, H., *On Violence* (Allen Lane, 1970).
COX, E., *Changing Aims in Religious Education* (Routledge and Kegan Paul, 1966).

COX, E., *Sixth-Form Religion* (S.C.M. Press, 1967).
ELLUL, J., *Violence* (S.C.M. Press, 1970).
GOLDMAN, R., *Religious Thinking from Childhood to Adolescence* (Routledge and Kegan Paul, 1964).
GOLDMAN, R., *Readiness for Religion* (Routledge and Kegan Paul, 1965).
HARE, R. M., *The Language of Morals* (O.U.P., 1952).
JEFFREYS, M. V. C., *Beyond Neutrality* (Pitman, 1955).
JEFFREYS, M. V. C., *Education – Christian or Pagan?* (Univ. of London Press, 1946).
JEFFREYS, M. V. C., *Religion and Morality* (R.E.P., 1967).
JEFFREYS, M. V. C., *Personal Values in the Modern World* (Penguin, 1962; rev. edition 1968).
LOUKES, H., *New Ground in Christian Education* (S.C.M. Press, 1965).
LOUKES, H., *Teenage Religion* (S.C.M. Press, 1961).
MACY, C. (ed.), *Let's Teach Them Right* (Pemberton Books, 1969).
MARITAIN, J., *True Humanism* (G. Bles, 1938).
MATHEWS, H. F., *Revolution in Religious Education* (R.E.P., 1966).
NIBLETT, W. R., *Christian Education in a Secular Society* (O.U.P., 1960).
NIBLETT, W. R. (ed.), *Moral Education in a Changing Society* (Faber and Faber, 1963).
PETERS, R. S., *Ethics and Education* (Allen and Unwin, 1966).
REID, L. A., *Creative Morality* (Allen and Unwin, 1937).
SMART, N., *Secular Education and the Logic of Religion* (Faber and Faber, 1968).
WHITEHEAD, A. N., *Religion in the Making* (C.U.P., 1926).
WILSON, J., *Moral Education and the Curriculum* (Pergamon, 1969).

Chapter 8
Conclusion

In the course of this book a number of problems have been examined: the relation of the individual and society, freedom and authority, continuity and change; and, underlying them all, the paradox or contradiction of human nature and destiny, pictured in the myths of Prometheus and Sisyphus, and in the Biblical story of the Fall of Man. Through the ages poets, dramatists, philosophers and theologians have been concerned with the mystery of man. Man, as Shelley wrote, 'having enslaved the elements remains himself a slave'. Reinhold Niebuhr reminds us[1] that Plato in the *Phaedo* describes the soul as 'opposing and coercing the elements of which she is believed to be composed ...', and adds: 'This inner conflict is an obvious fact which proves that man alone, among all animals, stands in contradiction to himself.' In the words of Christopher Fry: 'Tragedy is the demonstration of the human dilemma. Comedy is the comment on the human dilemma.' Augustine sums the matter up:[2] 'The true honour of man is the image and likeness of God, which is not preserved save in relation to Him by whom it is impressed ... But through the desire to make trial of his own power, man at his own bidding falls down to himself ...' Man likes to think of himself as the Lord of Creation. And he has been described as 'the filthiest animal on earth'.

This contradictory human creature is the material of education. And a vital part of education is to gain some insight into the mystery of human nature and destiny. Intellectual speculation is not in everyone's nature. It is not here suggested that everyone should have an explicitly formulated system of metaphysics – especially as metaphysics are somewhat out of fashion anyway. Some people express their philosophy in their attitudes and behaviour rather than in exposition. Our acquaintance with someone will show us whether, for example, his ultimate attitude towards the natural world is one of reverence or of exploitation. At some level of consciousness we have to come to terms with Reality. In our living, if not in our thinking, we must know whether, or why, we care about Reality, and whether Reality cares about us. Is our relation with Reality in some sense a living – even a personal – one? Or is Reality so much extended dead material amongst which we are, so to speak, 'on our own',

---
[1] *Nature and Destiny of Man*, I, p. 32.
[2] *De Trin.*, XII, xi, 16.

like astronauts in a capsule? If we can help people to come to terms with these questions, remote as they may seem from our mundane concerns, we shall be helping them to grow in stature as responsible persons. We shall, in short, be educating them.

Education must include some insight into the nature of thought and knowledge. There is value, as we have seen earlier, in distinguishing different kinds of thinking and knowing, though we should also appreciate that, in the last analysis, mental activity is one, and truth is one. Intuitive and conceptual knowing are not ultimately separate. Factual statements and value-judgements in the last resort both rest on the coherence and comprehensiveness of evidence. The argument for belief in God, and for the law of expansion of gases, is ultimately of the same nature. And, as Michael Polanyi has argued, all knowing involves personal participation.

Not only should education include insight into the nature of knowledge, but it should also include some grasp of the map of human knowledge – a coherent picture of the world.

Again, the business of education is not only intellectual. There must be opportunity for the exercise of responsible choice – that is to say, action according to considered opinion – and also for the acquisition of skills. An educated person not only knows how to think and where to get knowledge, but also can act in accordance with that thought and knowledge. There is, as we have seen, a paradox or dilemma in the relation between thought and action, inasmuch as we constantly have to act on inadequate grounds. Time will not wait, events have to be met, decisions have to be made. At the same time we must be prepared to re-think even our deepest convictions. It is comparatively easy to act positively with an obstinately closed mind, or to reconsider all our ideas in a state of permanent indecision. What is difficult is to combine the two virtues: to be able to act positively when action is needed, and at the same time to be prepared always to believe that we may be mistaken.

The third educational objective mentioned above is skill. An educated person is one who can do some things very well, and perhaps at least one thing very well indeed. It matters little in what field of activity the mastery is achieved; it may be athletic, musical, constructional, verbal. The acquisition of a skill is educational because it needs perseverance and selective discipline; it establishes its possessor among his fellows, and helps to build his own self-respect. The value of skill has been celebrated in a story by Anatole France, *Le Jongleur de Notre Dame*. Brother Barnabas was a simple, unlettered man, who felt at a disadvantage among his fellows in the monastery because he could not write books, copy manuscripts, perform chemical experiments, or carve figures of saints. He had no gifts to offer to Our Lady. But one day it was noticed that

Brother Barnabas was in the habit of disappearing into the chapel at a time when no one else was there. Moved by curiosity, the Father Prior and two senior monks went to the chapel and peered through the chinks in the door. They saw Brother Barnabas standing on his head, juggling with six copper balls and a dozen knives. He offered to Our Lady the best that he had. And when the Prior and his companions were about to enter and remove Brother Barnabas whom they judged insane, they saw the figure of Our Lady descend the steps and wipe the sweat from the juggler's brow with a fold of her azure robe.

At the risk of repetition it may be worth while to end with a final caution against overlooking the existential quality in all experience, and therefore in all learning. Books are written about education, and some of them are read. The very fact that we are sitting back and thinking about these things suggests that these things can be understood by sitting back and thinking. That indeed is part of the business of understanding; and there is a kind of understanding that can be attained without participation, and which has its own kind of clarity – the clarity gained by holding an object at arm's length. But full understanding is impossible without participation. The only way to learn is by living. By all means let us live with our eyes warily open, and look before we leap. But, if we want to be whole people, and not shadows, we must be involved in the business of living. Or, to put the same thing differently, in the words of Montaigne: 'We may become learned from the learning of others; wise we can never be except by our own wisdom.'[1]

[1] *Essays*, I, ch. 24.

Index

Acland, R., 115
Adams, Sir John, 48
Advertise (-ment), 7
Allport, G. W., 43
Alves, C., 115
America (-n), 11, 18, 33–4, 43, 54, 65, 98
Animal (-s), 8, 44–5, 57, 63, 75, 87, 90, 103, 112, 117
Aquinas, Thomas, 18 n., 47–8, 111
Archambault, R. D., 5
Arendt, H., 100 n., 115
Aristotle, 2, 8, 15, 26, 48, 71, 90
Art, 77–9
Ash, M., 72
Ashcroft, D., 36
Athens, Athenian, 16, 26
Augustine, 16, 48, 84, 110, 117
Authority, xi, 3, 21, 24, 28, 31–2, 36–7, 47 n., 56, 58, 95, 97, 99, 113, 117
Ayer, A. J., 85, 96
Ayerst, D., 72

Bacon, Francis, 71
Bantock, G. H., 4–5, 23, 41, 96
Barnes, K., 57
Barth, Karl, 110
Behaviourism, 84
Bentham, Jeremy, vii, 48, 86–7
Bergson, Henri, 84
Berlin, Sir Isaiah, 24, 29, 41
Beveridge, Sir William, 12
Bible (see also *New Testament*), 106–7, 117
Blishen, E., 56 n., 72
Bonhoeffer, D., 105, 107
Borger, R., 72
Bottomore, T. B., 23
Bouquet, Dr A. C., 95
Bowdler, Miss H., 101
Bray, J., 10 n.

Brearley, M., 55
Brougham, Lord, xi
Brown, J. A. C., 72
Brubacher, J. S., 5, 16 n., 23
Buber, Martin, 9, 23
Bühler, Charlotte, 49, 55
Bull, Dr N. J., 93–4, 96
Bultmann, Dr R., 105–7
Burke, Edmund, 110

Camus, A., 104
Carmichael, L., 55
Censorship, 26, 101
Change, 3, 42, 44, 52–3, 56, 97
Chivalry, 35
Christ (-ian) (-ianity), 3, 15 n., 16, 18, 26, 30, 38, 77, 80–1, 90, 98, 101, 103–13, 115
Choice, 11–12, 24–5, 28–9, 43, 84, 118
Church, 16–17, 28, 35
Cicero, 2
Citizen (-ship), 21, 26, 28, 33–4, 47 n.
Civilization, 4, 45–6, 50, 64, 98, 101
Clarke, Sir F., 41, 58
Clegg, Sir Alec, 51
Colleges of Education, 1–3, 52
Collier, K. G., 23
Collingwood, R. G., 47
Comenius, 35
Communication (-s), 8, 76
Communism, 17, 28, 33
Community, communities: see Society
Computer, 52
Conflict, 2–4, 7, 9, 10, 20, 24–5, 57, 97, 100, 112, 117
Continuity, 3, 42–4, 52–3, 56
Cox, E., 116
Cranston, M., 41
Creation, creative, 4, 31, 44, 57, 65, 74, 103–4, 106, 111, 117

Cromwell, Oliver, 83
Crowther Report (1959), 72
Curriculum, 56-7, 63, 65-7, 69, 71-2

Dalton Plan, 65
Darling, Dr F. F., 98
Darwin, Charles, 48
Democracy, xii, 14, 17, 21, 25, 27-8, 32, 34, 45-6, 50
Determinism, 24
Dewey, John, 20, 23, 34, 47-9, 55, 65
Discipline, 31, 35, 61, 65, 95
Disraeli, Benjamin, 22, 58
Douglas, J. W. B., 23
Durkheim, E., 96

Education (-al), xi-xii, 1-2, 4-5, 11, 14, 16, 18, 33-5, 37, 40, 43, 47-8, 50-54, 56-61, 64, 71-2, 74, 79, 101, 109, 113, 115, 117, 119
Education Act (1944), 35, 50
  Adult, 54
  Comprehensive, 35, 39, 51
  Elementary, xi, 50-1
  Higher, xi, 1, 20, 36, 51-2
  Liberal, xii, 69-71
  Primary, 19, 52, 61
  Secondary, xi, 20, 35, 50, 51-2, 66
  Vocational, xii, 19, 70; see also School
Eliot, T. S., 4 n., 40 n., 41
Ellul, J., 100 n., 108, 114, 116
Elvin, H. L., 5, 23
Environment, 4, 42-3, 46, 48-9, 62
Eppel, E. M. and E., 96
Erikson, E. H., 23
Ethical, Ethics: see *Moral*
Evolution, 48
Ewing, A. C., 96
Examinations, 19, 51-2, 57, 62
Existentialism, Existentialist, 3, 104, 119
Fact, Ch. 6 *passim*, esp. 82 ff.
Family, Families, xi, 8, 16, 21, 39-41
Farmington Trust, 93
Faust, 59-60
Fear, 37
Feeling, Ch. 6 *passim*, 79, 85
Fellowship, 9, 38
Feltre, Vittorino da, 2

Feudalism, 27
Flavell, J. H., 55
Fleming, C. M., 72
Floud, J. E., 23
Forster, W. E., 51
France, Anatole, 118
France, French, 18-19, 33, 66, 98
Frankenstein, 60
Free (-dom), 3, 9, 24-5, 28-32, 35-7, 44, 56, 58, 61, 84, 92, 95, 99-100, 104, 111-13, 115, 117
Freewill, 24
Freud, Anna, 49
Froebel, F., 19, 35, 43, 47, 49
Fry, Christopher, 117
Furneaux, W. D., 23

Garforth, F. W., 23
Germany, 66
Gesell, A. and B., 49
God, 17, 48, 64, 82, 84, 91-2, 97, 99, 102-3, 105, 107, 109-12, 118
Goethe, 60
Goldman, R., 116
Government, 10, 21, 26-8, 33-4, 36, 109
Graeco-Roman, 4, 16, 38
Greek, 104-5, 112
Grow (-th), 4, 9, 16, 20, 22, 42-4, 47-9, 53, 59

Hadfield, J. A., 55
Hadow Report (1926), 50
Halsey, A. H., 23
Hardie, C. D., 5
Harvard Report (1945), 70
Hebrew, Hebrew-Christian, 4, 97-8
Hegel, 47 n.
Helvétius, 43
Hilgard, E. R., 72
History, historical, xi-xii, 18, 33, 44-7, 50-2, 63, 76, 83, 86, 89, 97, 103-4, 106, 109-11
Holland, 19
Hollins, T. H. B., 5
Homer, 111
Hudson, W. D., 23
Human, human being, 8, 25, 28, 101

Humanism, 18 n., 110–11

Individual (-ity), 3, 7, 9, 11, 13, 16–22, 24, 29–30, 40, 43–5, 47, 53, 56, 61, 63, 117
Indoctrination, 115
Industrial Revolution, 19, 27, 50, 70
Intelligence, 23, 49, 93, 98
Isaacs, Susan 49, 55

Jacks, M. L., 5
Jeffreys, M. V. C., 5, 41, 116
Jesus: see Christ
Joint Examination Boards, 2
Judges, A. V., 5

Kant, I., 9, 91
Kay, W., 96
Kay-Shuttleworth, Sir James, 2
Keats, J., 78
Kerr, Clark, 54
Kilpatrick, W. H., 55, 65, 72
Knowledge, 56, 59–60, 62–5, 67, 71–2, 98, 112, 118
   Kinds of (existential or intuitive and conceptual), 74–8, 81

Laissez-faire. 27
Lamarck, 48
Lawton, Dr D., 68–9
Leach, Dr E., 38 n.
Learn (-ing), 4, Ch. 5 *passim*, esp. 57–63
Lejeune, A., 32
Leonard, G. B., 59–60
Lippmann, W., 33
Literacy, the Three R's, 19–20, 50
Local education authorities, 3
Locke, John, 18
Loukes, H., 116
Love, 4, 8–9, 37, 91, 99, 104–5; see also Fellowship
Lowe, Dr John, 54–5
Luther, Martin, 13, 31

McCallister, W. J., 41
McDougall, William, 82, 85
McNair Report, 1–3
Macy, C., 116

Man, 4, 8, 18, 30–1, 44–7, 49, 59, 76, 103–4, 109–12, 114, 117
Maritain, Jacques, 18 n., 23, 111–12, 116
Marlowe, Christopher, 60
Marriage, 44, 101
Marx, Karl, 31
Mathews, H. F., 116
Matthews, Dr W. R., 105
Mead, M., 23
Mechanization, 29
Melbourne, Lord, xi
Middle Ages, 16, 35
Mill, J. S., 30, 48, 87
Milton, John, xii, 5
Montaigne, 119
Montefiiore, A., 96
Montessori, Maria, 49
Moral (-ity), moral obligation, xii, 9, 13–14, 34–5, 60, 87–91, 93–5, 97–101, 109–10, 112–14
Morley, Lord, 80
Morris, D., 61 n.
Morrish, I., 5, 55
Moses, 98
Muggeridge, Malcolm, 98
Musgrove, P. W., 23

Neville, R., 28 n.
Newsom Report, 22
New Testament, 106–7, 110, 112–13
Newton, Sir Isaac, 83–4, 104
Niblett, W. R., 116
Niebuhr, Reinhold, 110, 117
Norwood, Cyril, vii

Oakes, P., 38
Olson, W. C., 72
Opinion, public, 10–11, 22, 26
Organism, 42–3, 47, 47 n.
Ottaway, A. K. C., 23
Oundle, 53

Paedeia, 16
Parents, 1, 38–9, 43, 97
Parkhurst, Helen, 65
Paul, St, 16, 30–1, 38, 40, 57, 87, 103, 106–7, 113
Peel, E. A., 55
Pei, M., 77 n., 96

Pericles, 16
Permissive (-ness), 11, 37, 99, 102
Person (-al), personality, 7, 9, 16, 22, 34, 42, 44, 51, 81 95–6, 106, 114, 118
Pestalozzi, J. H., 19, 35, 47
Peters, R. S., 5, 37 n., 41, 96, 116
Peterson, A. D. C., 71–2
Pharisees, 98, 102
Philosopher (-s), philosophy, 1, 3, 5, 18–19, 48–9, 63, 68, 76, 86, 92–3, 117
Piaget, J., 19, 49, 55, 96
Pinsent, A., 72
Plato, 2, 15, 35, 40, 48, 60, 87, 112, 117
Pleasure, 86–7, 89
Plowden Report, 61 n., 80
Polanyi, M., 41, 96 n.
Pollution, 46, 91
Popper, K. R., 23
Positivism, logical, 14, 85
Pragmatic, pragmatism, 48
Pring, R. A., 63 n., 66 n.
Progress, 4, 15
Prometheus, 117
Proof, 63–4, 91
Propaganda, 7, 58, 115
Prussia, 2, 19
Psychology, 1, 35, 43, 49, 59, 93

Quakers, 32
Quintilian, 2

Radcliffe, P., 41
Rational (-ist), 9, 18, 29, 71
Reason, 10, 18, 48, 82–3, 110, 112–3
Reeves, M. E., 55
Reformation, 18
Reid, L. A., 6, 96, 116
Reid, T. Wemyss, 51 n.
Religion, 51, 67, 78, 83, 94, 96–7, 99–100, 109–15
Renaissance, 17
Responsible, responsibility, 9, 24, 28–9, 36–7, 43, 49, 90–1, 94, 115
Robbins Report, 3
Robespierre, 33
Robinson, Dr J., 105, 107
Rome, Roman, 16–17, 109
Ross, J. S., 6

Rossetti, D. G., 77 n.
Rousseau, J. J., 9, 19, 25, 30, 32–3, 35, 47
Rusk, R. R., 6
Russia, 33, 65

Sanderson, F. W., 53
Sandström, C. I., 55
Scheffler, I., 6, 96
School (-s), xi-xii, 1, 14, 18, 20–2, 36–7, 39, 47, 52–3, 56, 62–4
Schools Council, 66, 72–3
Science (-s), 46, 59, 63, 70, 76–7, 80, 82–5, 95, 99; see also Technology
Sex, 11, 26, 99, 101, 103
Shaw, Bernard, 48 n.
Shelley, P. B., 60, 117
Sisyphus, 3, 117
Smart, Professor, N., 107, 116
Social, society, xi, 3–4, 7–9, 11–18, 20–22, 24, 26, 30, 32, 34, 36, 39, 44–50, 52, 56, 62–3, 67–8, 97, 108, 114, 117
Social Services, 12
Sociology, 1, 43, 83, 93
Socrates, 15, 111
Sophists, 15
Sophocles, 111
Sparta, 26
Specialist, specialism, 35 n., 64
Spencer, Herbert, 20
Stapledon, O., 87 n.
State, the 10, 20, 26–7, 31, 41, 47 n., 115
   Welfare State, 12, 17, 27, 29, 39, 45
Stead, Dr H. G., 60
Stoics, 25
Stones, E., 2
Sturt, Dr M., 80 n.
Subject (-s), 56, 63, 65, 67–9, 79
Sugarman, B., 93
Swiss, Switzerland, 19

Teacher (-s), xii, 1–2, 21, 37–40, 52, 56, 58–9, 60–2, 66, 69, 72, 81, 93
Teaching, 56–7, 64, 115
Technical, technology, technological, 2–4, 11, 17, 46, 51, 59, 98–9, 110

Theology, 3, 17, 91, 93, 99, 103–5, 107–8, 112, 117
Thompson, Francis, 102 n.
Thomson, G. H., 6
Thomson, R., 72
Thorpe, L. P., 55
Tibble, J. W., 6
Tillich, P., 105–6
Time, 84
Toulmin, S., 96
Toynbee, A. J., 45
Tradition, 4, 40, 97
Training, 1–2
Training Colleges: see Colleges of Education
Truth, 63–4, 74, 80, 82, 92, 111, 113–14

University (-ies), xi, 2–3, 36, 40, 52, 54, 63, 66
Utilitarian (-ism), 48, 86, 88

Valentine, C. W., 55
Value (-s), xi, 33–4, 48–9, 74, 81–2, 85–7, 92–3, 95–8, 118
Virgil, 111
Vietnam, 11
Violence, 100, 114
Voluntary agencies, 26, 54 n.

Wells, H. G., xi
Wheeler, D. K., 72
Whitehead, A. N., 6, 54, 70, 114, 116
Whitman, Walt, vii, 103
Wilkes, K., 96
Williams, N., 93
Wilson, Colin, 28 n.
Wilson, John, 93, 96, 116
Wiseman, S., 23
Wollstonecraft, M., 60
Woozley, A. D., 96

Yudkin, M., 71 n., 72